Homiletics from the HEART

Preaching God's Word God's Way

Dr. John Goetsch

Revival Books and
West Coast Baptist College
A ministry of Lancaster Baptist Church
4020 E. Lancaster Blvd.
Lancaster, CA 93535
661-946-2274
www.westcoastbaptist.edu
E-mail: wcbaptist@aol.com

Copyright ©2003

Cover design and layout by Craig Parker

All rights reserved. No part of this book may be reproduced or transmitted in any form or by any means, electronic or mechanical, including photocopying, recording, or any information storage and retrieval system, without written permission.

ISBN 0-9726506-2-8

Printed and bound in the United States of America.

To the young men whom I have had the privilege of teaching homiletics at West Coast Baptist College—past, present, and future.

Contents

Introduction vii

Chapter One - *Called to Preach* 1
Chapter Two - *Choosing the Scripture* 17
Chapter Three - *Collecting the Facts* 31
Chapter Four - *Constucting the Introduction* 37
Chapter Five - *Creating an Outline* 49
Chapter Six - *Challenging Through Illustrations* 63
Chapter Seven - *Convicting Conclusions* 79
Chapter Eight - *Compassionate Delivery* 85
Chapter Nine - *Conducting the Invitation* 99
Chapter Ten - *Character of Preachers* 109
Chapter Eleven - *Controlled by the Holy Spirit* 125
Conclusion 137

Appendix I - *The Putting Off - Putting On Principle* 145
Appendix II - *How to Memorize Scripture* 159

Notes 175
Bibliography 179

Introduction

In the summer of 1971, I took a job on a farm near Gilman, Wisconsin. My dad had sold our farm during my senior year of high school, so this job was going to be a natural. It was a typical dairy farm with acres of corn and alfalfa fields. My "boss", Everett Hettinger, was an ex-Marine who took life and work seriously. There were many things that displeased him, but one in particular created an experience I will never forget. One of the alfalfa fields had become "home" to a large number of foxes, who never seemed to tire of digging holes and thus rooting up the alfalfa crop. This infuriated Mr. Hettinger and wiping out those foxes became one of his lifelong passions.

One night, around 11:00 p.m., he handed me a shotgun and said, "C'mon, we're going after them!" I tried to explain to him that I had never shot a gun in my life. (My mother was against guns and my dad was not a hunter) But nothing was going to deter this man from his mission. He instructed me to climb up in the back of his old pick-up truck with the gun. He slowly drove that pick-up with the headlights off out to the field where the foxes were. Suddenly, he spotted one! He flipped the headlights on and floored the accelerator. I could barely hang on as we flew across that hay field in the middle of the night. We got within fifty feet of that poor fox, when Mr. Hettinger started screaming, "Shoot him!" I said, "Do what?" He said, "Aim the gun and shoot!" The gun had been the least of my worries, as I was desperately trying to simply stay on board that bouncing truck. Laying across the back of that cab, I pointed that gun toward the furry red creature that was zig-zagging his way through the alfalfa. My boss was now yelling, "Pull the trigger now, you idiot!" At forty miles an hour, I couldn't keep my body still much less aim that gun. But finally, figuring it was either me or the fox that was going to get shot that night, I closed my eyes and squeezed the trigger. As the echo of that blast resounded through the grove of trees nearby, suddenly everything stopped. When I opened my eyes, the truck had stopped, Mr. Hettinger had stopped yelling, and the little red fox lay motionless on the ground. In one perfect shot, I had nailed my first hunting trophy! I put his tail on the antenna of my Corvair to display for everyone my expert hunting skills.

The next day I asked Mr. Hettinger if I could borrow his guns. I was convinced this hunting thing was a piece of cake.

For the next several weeks, every time I got a free moment I was shooting those guns. You know what? I couldn't hit a tin can on a fence post from twenty feet! I soon gave up and to this day have never shot anything again.

Growing up in a good church, I always knew that there was something very special about the preaching of God's Word. I was saved as a result of an evangelistic message on the subject of Hell and many times before and after my conversion had felt the conviction of the Holy Spirit that accompanied preaching. But I always thought that anybody who wanted to could preach. I mean, how hard could it be to simply stand up and say what God had already said?

Those thoughts, however, evaporated quickly the day I was given my first opportunity to preach. I spent my second summer of college as an intern at the Woodcrest Baptist Church in Minneapolis, Minnesota, under the leadership of Pastor Clarke Poorman. Every morning he would meet with me; and we would read and memorize Scripture, spend time in prayer, and then plan the day's activities. One particular morning, he mentioned that we would be conducting a service at a retirement home and that I would be doing the preaching. I protested with, "But I'm not called to preach—I haven't taken any classes yet in homiletics!" He said, "You have an hour to prepare—you'll do fine."

I recall going to the office next door, opening my Bible, and staring at the pages hoping that a sermon would pop into my mind. Thirty minutes passed and I had nothing. I decided maybe I should pray; and as I asked God for help, the thought of Heaven came to my mind. I thought to myself, "This is perfect, these people are old, they are about to die, what could be better than to preach on Heaven—they're almost there!" I decided on Psalm 23:6b as my text, "I will dwell in the house of the Lord forever."

I got about one minute into my five-minute sermon, when a ninety-one year old lady in a wheelchair on the front row raised her hand. I had never seen anyone ask a question in the middle of a message before, but I paused, looked at her and said, "Yes, can I help you?" She said in her feeble voice, "Is my mother going to be there?" I kindly tried to explain that if her mother had trusted Christ as her personal Saviour, then indeed she would be there in Heaven. I went on preaching, but within a few seconds, this same lady again raised her hand. Again, I paused and nodded to her and she asked, "Is my mother going to be there?" I said, "Like I said before, if she trusted Christ during her life, she will be in Heaven." I went on only to be interrupted a third time by her voice: "Is my mother going to be there?" Frustrated that this little old lady was ruining my first sermon, I moved over directly in front of her face and said, "Lady, if you don't put your hand down, and be quiet, you are going to be there!" I'm afraid that if Pastor Poorman had not rescued me, my first sermon would have resulted in the murder of a ninety-one year old lady.

Through that experience and many thereafter, I began to realize that the preparation and presentation of God's message are not as easy as they seem. Just as the athlete or musician spends many hours in practice prior to the game or performance, so the preacher must spend countless hours in preparation of his heart and message. Once prepared, the delivery of a sermon requires spiritual, mental, and physical energy that will leave the preacher literally exhausted. Dr. Richard Weeks, my homiletics teacher, used to tell us that preaching a single sermon was equivalent to working eight hours of manual labor. I have found that when God has burned into my heart His truth and has burdened my heart for the audience, he was exactly right—preaching is hard work!

I recall the first time a little girl asked me to sign her Bible after I had preached in the fall of 1972. Signing my autograph was easy, but I knew that it was customary for preachers to put a verse beneath their name. For some reason, II Timothy 4:1-8 came to my mind and since then I have always used those verses with my autograph. When God called me to preach, I knew that I had very little to offer God, but I knew that His Word was powerful and could change lives forever. I have asked God to let my preaching be dominated with His Word, rather than my opinion, my advice, or my experiences.

I love that admonition of Paul to Timothy, "Preach the word!" Preach means "to cry out, herald, or exhort." Haddon W. Robinson states, "Preaching should so stir a man that he pours out the message with passion and fervor. Not all passionate pleading from a pulpit, however, possesses divine authority. When a preacher speaks as a herald, he must cry out 'the word.' Anything less cannot legitimately pass for Christian preaching."[1]

Paul goes on to say in verse two of II Timothy chapter four, "… be instant in season, out of season; reprove, rebuke, exhort with all longsuffering and doctrine." Like a military officer, the aged apostle gives five important imperatives to young Timothy as he begins his ministry of preaching.

Readiness

The command to "be instant in season, out of season" carries the picture of a soldier on duty, ready for battle at any moment. Dr. B. Myron Cedarholm used to tell us as "preacher boys" in college to always be ready "to preach, pray, or die." Preaching is not something we do only when we feel like it or when the audience is receptive to our message. Later in verses three and four, Paul reminds us, "For the time will come when they will not endure sound doctrine; but after their own lusts shall they heap to themselves teachers, having itching ears; And they shall turn away their ears from the truth, and shall be turned unto fables." Harold T. Bryson reminds us that "the proclaimer of God's Word needs to stay with the task of preaching whether he feels like it or not.... The preacher must be faithful to preach the Word regardless of whether listeners welcome it, reject it, or ignore it."[2]

Reprove

The next imperative, to "reprove," applies to human reason. This word carries the idea of a lawyer cross-examining or questioning a witness. Refuting error or proving something wrong is a huge part of the preacher's responsibility. A few verses earlier in II Timothy 3:16, the Holy Spirit reminds us that the Word of God is "profitable… for reproof…" In Titus 1:9-11 we see that a preacher must be one who is "holding fast the faithful word as he hath been taught, that he may be able by sound doctrine both to exhort and to convince the gainsayers. For there are many unruly and vain talkers and deceivers, specially they of the circumcision: Whose mouths must be stopped, who subvert whole houses, teaching things which they ought not, for filthy lucre's sake." Ephesians 5:11 states,

"And have no fellowship with the unfruitful works of darkness, but rather reprove them." Bryson explains, "To reprove in preaching means to present the axioms of the Christian faith or to refute in a reasoned manner the errors marshaled against the faith."[3]

Rebuke

The verb "rebuke" in the first century referred to moral censure. When people turn from the truth of God's Word, often the next step is into sin. As preachers we must be willing to confront people with what the Bible says about their sin. In I Timothy 5:20, Paul stated, "Them that sin rebuke before all, that others also may fear." In Titus 1:12-13, he says, "…The Cretians are always liars, evil beasts, slow bellies. This witness is true. Wherefore rebuke them sharply, that they may be sound in the faith." Like Nathan of old, the preacher must be willing to expose sin and declare, "Thou art the man." Preaching must reach the conscience of a man if change is to take place.

Revive

The word "exhort" in our passage has a double meaning in that it means to "comfort" as well as to "urge." Many today are hurting in despair, discouragement, and disappointment. The preacher must revive the heart of the despondent with the Word of God. But he must also urge and persuade the apathetic to action. Reviving the indifferent to obedience is needed today in this Laodicean age of "going through the motions" and "comfort zone" Christianity. The need of this hour is revival and the preacher of God's Word must exhort

God's people to awaken out of their sleep and redeem the time.

Remain

Then Paul tells the preacher that he must do all of this with "all longsuffering and doctrine." Preaching requires a faithful patience. The seed must be sown, then watered, cultivated, fertilized, and in time harvested. James uses the farmer as our example in James 5:7-8, "…Behold, the husbandman waiteth for the precious fruit of the earth, and hath long patience for it, until he receive the early and the latter rain. Be ye also patient; stablish your hearts… ." As we are faithful, God promises to give the increase. "For as the rain cometh down, and the snow from heaven, and returneth not thither, but watereth the earth, and maketh it bring forth and bud, that it may give seed to the sower, and bread to the eater: So shall my word be that goeth forth out of my mouth: it shall not return unto me void, but it shall accomplish that which I please, and it shall prosper in the thing whereto I sent it." (Isaiah 55:10-11) No other endeavor in life promises those kinds of results!

Whether you are just starting out or whether you are a seasoned veteran of many years in the pulpit, it is my prayer that the pages of this book will serve as an encouragement and help to your ministry of preaching. "Anyone desiring to be a preacher must hear the imperative, 'Preach the Word!' and then begin to obey the mandate. Preaching the Word is the task of a born-again believer who has received a unique call of God. When God calls anyone to expound the Bible, He bestows the gift of expounding. God gives abilities to interpret, skills to communicate, and competence for speaking. But God's gifts do not come without human cooperation. The preacher must study the Bible, learn people's needs, develop communication skills, learn sermon organization skills, and develop constantly in the many areas of the preaching task. To preach the Word means to act as if everything in preaching depends on God and to work as if everything depends on the preacher. Preaching involves a pilgrimage full of glories, challenges, discouragements, delights, failures, improvements, and possibilities."[4]

"The message of the biblical preacher is the most important message in the world. It calls for an all-out human effort coupled with the supernatural moving of the Holy Spirit, in both preparation and presentation. This involves hard work. There is no substitute."[5] Preaching requires a 24/7 commitment. The message cannot be separated from the messenger. Thus, we have chosen as our title *Homiletics from the Heart*. Good food served with dirty hands is undesirable. The construction of our homiletics and the condition of our heart must be in harmony. It is possible to fail at being a Christian before we fail at being a preacher. Hopefully, the following pages will help to keep both our heart and our homiletics in good order.

As C. H. Spurgeon declared, "Every workman knows the necessity of keeping his tools in a good state of repair, for, if the iron be blunt, and he does not whet the edge, then must he put to more strength. If the workman lose the edge, he knows that there will be a greater draught upon his energies, or his work will be badly done. Michaelangelo, the elect of the fine arts, understood so well the importance of his tools, that he always made his own brushes with his own hands, and in this he gives us an illustration of the God of grace, who with special care fashions for himself all true ministers.... We shall be likely to accomplish most when we are in the best spiritual condition; or in other words, we shall usually do our Lord's work best when our gifts and graces are in good order, and we shall do worst when they are most out of trim."[6]

CHAPTER ONE

Called to Preach

Several years ago I picked up a brochure from an Episcopalian college. On the outside cover it asked this question: "Have you considered the vocation of the ministry?" Two very serious errors were made in the posing of that question. The ministry is neither a "consideration" nor a "vocation." Unlike secular occupations, the ministry is not a job that you choose to do to make a living. It is a call from God that will either be obeyed or disobeyed.

The Apostle Paul lived persecuting those who followed the Gospel until one day God intervened with a call to preach that Gospel. "But when it pleased God, who separated me from my mother's womb, and called me by his grace, To reveal his Son in me, that I might preach him among the heathen; immediately I conferred not with flesh and blood." (Galatians 1:15-16) Paul was perhaps the most unlikely candidate for the ministry, but God calls the unlikely in order to receive the glory. "For ye see your calling, brethren, how that not many wise men after the flesh, not many mighty, not many noble, are called: But God hath chosen the foolish things of the world to confound the wise; and God hath chosen the weak things of the world to confound the things which are mighty; And base things of the world, and things which are despised, hath God chosen, yea, and things which are not, to bring to nought things that are: That no flesh should glory in his presence. But of him are ye in Christ Jesus, who of God is made unto us wisdom, and righteousness, and sanctification, and redemption: That, according as it is written, He that glorieth, let him glory in the Lord." (I Corinthians 1:26-31)

If you are looking for a position of comfort or credit, then preaching is not for you. For though it may seem like that is the case—God can only use those who are willing to let God work through them. "It is the spirit that quickeneth; the flesh profiteth nothing: the words that I speak unto you, they are spirit and they are life." (John 6:63) If, however, you are looking for a task that will bring eternal results—then preaching is that task!

Has God called you to preach? Are you willing to do so if He does? While serving that internship in Minneapolis, I accompanied a group of teenagers to Ontario, Canada, on a mission's work trip. Out in the middle of seemingly nowhere, we cleared brush, built some rugged buildings, and held a Vacation Bible School for Indian children. During the morning and evening hours, we would take a break from our work and have chapel. As the Word of God was preached that week, God began to talk to me about His call upon my life. Early each morning, under great conviction to answer that call, I would go out by the lake and read my Bible and pray. I wanted to serve the Lord with my life, but the call to preach seemed so unrealistic. I was an introverted farm kid who hated speech in school. The most I could see myself doing in the ministry was perhaps coaching football or basketball in a Christian School.

I never walked an aisle that week or told anyone of God's work in my life. To me, this call was too serious and too sacred to take lightly. If God was indeed in this, He would have to do it, for I was totally incapable of such a task. Kneeling by a rock along side that lake, I told the Lord that if He was indeed calling me to preach, He would have to confirm it in my heart over and over again for the next six months. Call it a "fleece" if you like, but this was far too serious for me to have doubts about two weeks later. I wanted no part of the ministry without God. For those next six months it seemed like every time I read the Bible, heard preaching, or prayed, the only message I got was that God wanted me to preach! I never did go forward and declare my decision, but God was building a fire in my bones that was not going out. I was excited about a purpose for my life, but scared to death of the responsibility. Hundreds of times in the coming years, I would remind God of what He had written in I Thessalonians 5:24, "Faithful is he that calleth you, who also will do it."

Perhaps like me, you are skeptical or fearful of God's call in your life. I think you will find encouragement in some biblical examples. Don't be too surprised if you see yourself in one or more of these examples.

Biblical Examples of God's Call to Ministry

Moses—Exodus 3:1-15
Moses was shocked at God's call in his life. "And Moses said unto God, Who am I, that I should go unto Pharaoh, and that I should bring forth the children of Israel out of Egypt?" (verse 11) Anyone who struts around bragging about his call to preach is more than likely "self-called." The call to ministry is not about us, but about God working through us. Moses possessed neither training, or gifts, or reputation for leadership prior to this call. In verse ten of chapter four, Moses protested, "O my Lord, I am not eloquent, neither heretofore, nor since thou hast spoken unto thy servant: but I am slow of speech, and of a slow tongue." But God's presence and provision always accompany His call, for God responds to his protest by saying, "…Who hath made man's mouth? Or who maketh the dumb, or deaf, or the seeing, or the blind? have not I the Lord? Now therefore go, and I will be with thy mouth, and will teach thee what thou shalt say." (Exodus 4:11-12)

There are no acceptable excuses when God calls. "For the gifts and calling of God are without repentance" (Romans 11:29). "Being confident of this very thing, that he which hath begun a good work in you will perform it until the day of Jesus Christ." (Philippians 1:6) Your calling is no accident or mistake. God doesn't call according to your gifts, He gifts according to your call!

Samuel—I Samuel 3:1-11

God may call at a young age. Spiritual maturity and knowledge of the Bible are not necessarily a prerequisite. God can train after He calls. Dr. Paul Levin, a wonderful and mightily used evangelist, was called to preach shortly after his conversion at the age of four! God's call will be heard by those, who like Samuel, have a sensitive and obedient heart. If you are sensing His call—do not run from it. The consequences of disobedience are great—just ask Jonah! "...Today if ye will hear his voice, Harden not your heart." (Psalm 95:7-8) "Happy is the man that feareth alway: but he that hardenth his heart shall fall into mischief." (Proverbs 28:14)

It is not wrong to ask God to repeat His call in order to be sure, as long as we are not resistant in our heart. We may question the faith of Gideon as he places a fleece before the Lord on two occasions. But God answered the fleece! God was not displeased with Gideon for wanting to be sure of God's will for his life. The advice of Eli to Samuel will work today: "...Go, lie down: and it shall be, if he call thee, that thou shalt say, Speak, Lord; for thy servant heareth..." (I Samuel 3:9).

Amos—Amos 7:14-15

Amos was not from a long line of preachers in his family. "...I was no prophet, neither was I a prophet's son; but I was an herdman, and a gatherer of sycamore fruit." (Amos 7:14) I have often mentioned that I am not a "PK," that is, a Preacher's Kid. I am not an "MK," that is, a Missionary's Kid. I am a "CK," a Custodian's Kid! My parents were farmers who every Saturday voluntarily cleaned the church for the Lord's day. Now if your dad is a preacher, it is a wonderful thing to follow him into the ministry, but remember, we are not "Mama called and Papa sent." We are God called and God sent! He can call you from any background and provide for you regardless of your pedigree.

It is interesting to me that God usually calls someone to preach who is already busy doing something and is not afraid of work. "And the Lord took me as I followed the flock..." (Amos 7:15). God is not so desperate that He is checking daily the welfare rolls to see who needs something to do. The ministry is hard work and anyone who is afraid to roll up his sleeves will never make it. "This is a true saying, If a man desire the office of a bishop, he desireth a good work." (I Timothy 3:1) Paul reminds Timothy to "... do the work of an evangelist" in II Timothy 4:5.

Isaiah—Isaiah 6:1-8

After Isaiah had seen the holiness of God in verses one through four, recognized his own sinfulness in verse five, and heard God's plea for workers in verse eight; he responded with, "... Here am I; send me." God will take volunteers!

The need for men to preach the Gospel is great in the world today as it was in Jesus' day:

"But when he saw the multitudes, he was moved with compassion on them, because they fainted, and were scattered abroad, as sheep having no shepherd. Then saith he unto his disciples, The harvest truly is plenteous, but the labourers are few; Pray ye therefore the Lord of the harvest, that he will send forth labourers into the harvest." (Matthew 9:36-38) This is the only time God asks us to put something on our prayer list. He asks us to pray for labourers. I am convinced that if men would begin to pray for preachers, that God would answer that prayer by calling them!

Ezekiel—Ezekiel 3:4-11
The life of Ezekiel shows us that God's call does not guarantee reception or results. "But the house of Israel will not hearken unto thee; for they will not hearken unto me: for all the house of Israel are impudent and hardhearted." (Ezekiel 3:7) But God does promise strength according to the task. "Fear them not, neither be dismayed at their looks, though they be a rebellious house." (Ezekiel 3:9) "So the spirit lifted me up, and took me away, and I went in bitterness, in the heat of my spirit; but the hand of the Lord was strong upon me." (Ezekiel 3:14)

Regardless of the circumstances or the outcome, God promises, "... My grace is sufficient for thee; for my strength is made perfect in weakness... ." (II Corinthians 12:9) "But unto every one of us is given grace according to the measure of the gift of Christ." (Ephesians 4:7) Where God guides, He always provides!

Peter, Andrew, James, and John—Matthew 4:18-22
From the call of God in these men, we see the priority of God's work over man's work. Their response to God was immediate. They were willing to leave everything—occupation, family, etc. They got into trouble when they went back to those things—see John 21:3.

So, what are you waiting for? Is God calling you? No excuses will pass at the judgment bar of God. He's not making a mistake—you are, if you refuse! Remember, God's calling brings with it an equipping and an anointing for the task. As one great leader has stated, "We have nothing to fear but fear itself!"

Basic Requirements for a God-Called Preacher

"Preaching is more than a craft or an art or a profession. It is more than the shaping of some words designed to dazzle the ears of hearers. Preaching grows out of the minister's own experience with the living God. As preachers, we stand inside faith. We are not objective. We bear witness to what has changed our lives.

A key word is relationship. Preaching cannot be separated from all that a minister is. The concept that we just "get up" a sermon fails to take seriously all of the factors that converge in the person who is preaching. Preaching cannot be separated from the person of the preacher."[7]

Dr. James Stalker, in his lectures on preaching at Yale in 1891 stated, "The outer must be preceded by the inner; public life for God must be preceded by private life with God; unless God has first spoken to man, it is vain for a man to attempt to speak for God.... . Before he begins to make God known, he should first himself know God."[8]

In February of 1872, Henry Ward Beecher, also at Yale, addressed students with these words, "There is no theology in the world that is anything more than an instrument. It is a mere tool to work with, an artillery to fight with. Sermons are mere tools; and the business that you have in hand is not making sermons, or preaching sermons, it is saving men. Let this come up before you so frequently that it shall never be forgotten, that none of these things should gain ascendancy over this prime controlling element of your lives, that you are to save men.

"And the first thing you have to do is to present to them what you want them to be. That is, if you are to preach to them faith, the best definition you can give of faith is to exercise it. If you wish to teach them the nature of sympathy, take them by the hand. Talk with the young men, and let them get acquainted with you; and they will soon find out what sympathy means. If you would explain what true benevolence is, be yourselves before them that which you want them to understand and imitate. What does the apostle tell us? 'Ye are our epistles, known and read of all men.' A minister is a live man… . If anywhere else he is deficient, he cannot be deficient in heart."[9]

No preacher can "hide behind the cross" as he preaches. The minister is as much the message as the sermon. A preacher was once asked, "How long did it take you to write that message?" His response was, "All of my life." Indeed, the two are inseparable. Before we can learn how to preach, we must learn how to live. To preach well requires one to live well. C.H. Spurgeon in his lecture on "The Minister's Self-Watch" quotes Robert Murray McCheyne, "How diligently the cavalry officer keeps his sabre clean and sharp; every stain he rubs off with the greatest care. Rememnber you are God's sword, His instrument—I trust, a chosen vessel unto Him to bear His name. In great measure, according to the purity and perfection of the instrument, will be the success. It is not great talents God blesses so much as likeness to Jesus. A holy minister is an awful weapon in the hand of God."[10]

The Preacher Must Be Converted
No one can effectively distribute the truth of the Gospel without first being a partaker himself. Now God's hand could be on a man before salvation, as was the case with Samuel, or even before birth, as was the case with John the Baptist. Judas Iscariot participated in the ministry without

being saved to be sure—but it only makes common sense that before one can effectively preach Christ, he must know Christ. "I am the vine, ye are the branches: He that abideth in me, and I in him, the same bringeth forth much fruit: for without me ye can do nothing." (John 15:5) Spurgeon stated, "Better to abolish pulpits than fill them with men who have no experimental knowledge of what they teach."[11]

The Pharisees of Jesus' day were examples of an outward pretense without inward possession of the truth. "Woe unto you, scribes and Pharisees, hypocrites! for ye make clean the outside of the cup and of the platter, but within they are full of extortion and excess. Thou blind Pharisee, cleanse first that which is within the cup and platter, that the ouside of them may be clean also. Woe unto you, scribes and Pharisees, hypocrites! for ye are like unto whited sepulchres, which indeed appear beautiful outward, but are within full of dead men's bones, and of all uncleanness. Even so ye also outwardly appear righteous unto men, but within ye are full of hypocrisy and iniquity. Ye serpents, ye generation of vipers, how can ye escape the damnation of hell?" (Matthew 23:25-28, 33)

Gregory admonished, "The hand that means to make another clean, must not itself be dirty." Spurgeon spared no words on this matter, "How horrible to be a preacher of the gospel and yet to be unconverted! Let each man here whisper to his own inmost soul, 'What a dreadful thing it will be for me if I should be ignorant of the power of the truth which I am preparing to proclaim!' Unconverted ministry involves the most unnatural relationships. A graceless pastor is a blind man elected to a professorship of optics, philosophizing upon light and vision, discoursing upon and distinguishing to others the nice shades and delicate blendings of the prismatic colours, while he himself is absolutely in the dark! He is a dumb man elevated to the chair of music; a deaf man fluent upon symphonies and harmonies! He is a mole professing to educate eaglets; a limpet elected to preside over angels."[12]

The Preacher Must Be Committed
The call to preach is a life-long commitment. This is not something we try for awhile to see how we will do or how it will treat us. "The gifts and calling of God are without repentance"—God doesn't change His mind! "... No man having put his hand to the plough, and looking back, is fit for the kingdom of God." (Luke 9:62) The Apostle Paul focused on one thing—his calling of God, "Brethren, I count not myself to have apprehended: but this one thing I do, forgetting those things which are behind, and reaching forth unto those things which are before, I press toward the mark for the prize of the high calling of God in Christ Jesus." (Philippians 3:13-14)

In a dingy, dirty, six-dollar-a-night motel room in downtown Los Angeles in 1976, I made a commitment to the ministry. My revival meeting for that week had been canceled. I had nowhere to go for six days and after paying for my motel room for the week, I had just two dollars in my pocket. I had no gas in my car, no friends to call on, and the television in my room got only "snow." But it was there, alone with God in fasting and prayer, that I made a commitment to Him to preach regardless of the cost. That week may have been the best "meeting" I ever held in all the years of evangelism, for it produced a decision in my own heart of commitment to God's call.

The Preacher Must Be Consecrated
The preacher's life must be free from the "baggage" of this world. "And let every one that nameth the name of Christ depart from iniquity. But in a great house there are not only vessels of gold and of silver, but also of wood and of earth; and some to honour, and some to dishonour. If a man therefore purge himself from these, he shall be a vessel unto honour, sanctified, and meet for the master's use, and prepared unto every good work." (II Timothy 2:19-21)

I love the taste of a cold Diet Coke! Never once, however, have I come home thirsty, taken ice cubes and placed them in the dog's dish, and filled it with Diet Coke and quenched my thirst! The dog's dish is a vessel of dishonor, it is not fit for human use. I choose rather a clean glass from the cupboard—one that has been carefully washed with soap and water. God desperately needs preachers today, but He will only use a clean vessel.

When God lists His qualifications for ministers, He uses a most interesting word—"blameless." "A bishop then must be blameless, the husband of one wife, vigilant, sober, of good behavior, given to hospitality, apt to teach; Not given to wine, no striker, not greedy of filthy lucre; but patient, not a brawler, not covetous; One that ruleth well his own house, having his children in subjection with all gravity; (For if a man know not how to rule his own house, how shall he take care of the church of God?) Not a novice, lest being lifted up with pride he fall into the condemnation of the devil. Moreover he must have a good report of them that are without; lest he fall into reproach and the snare of the devil." (I Timothy 3:2-7) Again, in Titus 1:7 he uses that same word, "For a bishop must be blameless, as the steward of God... ." The word "blameless" here does not mean "perfect" but rather means "without handles." There must be nothing in our lives that someone can grab onto and pull us or the Gospel message down.

In and of itself, it would not be sinful for a preacher to walk into a liquor store and buy a Pepsi. But if an unsaved man were to see the preacher walking into the liquor store as he drove by not knowing his reason for doing so, that preacher would no longer be blameless in his eyes. He would have a handle that could be used as a stumbling block to his conversion. The higher one goes in leadership, the more narrow the road becomes!

The Preacher Must Be In Communion With God
Someone who is called to preach must be in a growing relationship with God. Paul's desire was, "That I may know him, and the power of his resurrection, and the fellowship of his sufferings, being made conformable unto his death." (Philippians 3:10) Of Enoch, the Bible simply says, "And Enoch walked with God." (Genesis 5:24) What a testimony! What a legacy! What an influence!

One night after my mother heard me preach, she said, "John, when will preachers stop working up their sermons in their heads and start praying down their messages from God?" I never asked her if she was referring to me, but her words cut to the quick! To preach Christ we must know Christ. Our audience will be able to tell whether our sermon came from God or our library shelves!

Is the preacher perfect? Not by a long shot! (David, Jonah, Elijah, Peter, Thomas, Apollos, and Paul are all examples of imperfect instruments.) But to be a preacher, one has to be out in front of those he is trying to lead in his personal walk with God. He is a sinner saved by grace but growing in that grace daily. It would be a waste of time for me to write and for you to read the following chapters on homiletics if we do not take heed to this chapter on the condition of our heart. Preaching is "truth" and "personality." They cannot be separated, but rather the messenger and the message must be in perfect harmony to achieve God's results.

Before we get into the "nuts and bolts" of homiletics, I want to challenge you to read the following excerpts taken from an ordination charge given by Dr. James Stalker. It was delivered at the ordination service in Gallatown, Kirkcaldy, in 1879 for the Rev. William Agnew.

"Perhaps there is no profession which so thoroughly as ours tests and reveals what is in a man—the stature of his manhood, the mass and quality of his character, the poverty or richness of his mind, the coldness or warmth of his spirituality. These all come out in our work, and become known to our congregation and the community in which we labour.

"It seems to me to lie at the very root of a right ministerial life to be possessed with this idea—to get quit of everything like pretence and untruthfulness, to wish for no success to which one is not entitled, and to look upon elevation into any position for which one is unfit as a pure calamity.

"The man's self—the very thing he is, standing with his bare feet on the bare earth—this is the great concern. This is the self to which you are to take heed—what you really are, what you are growing into, what you may yet become.

"All our work is determined by this—the spirit and power of our preaching, the quality of the influence we exert, and the tenor of our walk and conversation. We can no more rise above ourselves than water can rise above its own level… What is in us must come out, and nothing else. All we say and do is merely the expression of what we are.

"Evidently, therefore, there can be nothing so important as carefully to watch over our inner life, and see that it be large, sweet and spiritual, and that it be growing.

"Yet the temptations to neglect and overlook this and turn our attention in other directions are terribly strong. The ministerial life is a very outside life; it is lived in the glare of publicity; it is always pouring out. We are continually preaching, addressing meetings, giving private counsel, attending public gatherings, going from home, frequenting church courts, receiving visits, and occupied with details of every kind. We live in a time when all men are busy, and ministers are the busiest of men. From Monday morning till Sunday night the bustle goes on continually.

"This is what we have to fight against. The people we live among and the hundreds of details of our calling will steal away our inner life altogether, if they can. And then, what is our outer life worth? It is worth nothing. If the inner life get thin and shallow, the outer life must become a perfunctory discharge of duties. Our preaching will be empty, and our conversation and intercourse unspiritual.

"We must find time for reading, study, meditation and prayer. We should at least insist on having a large forenoon, up, say, to two o'clock every day, clear of interruptions. These hours of quietness are our real life! It is these that make the ministerial life a grand life. When we are shut in alone, and, the spirit having been silenced and collected by prayer, the mind gets slowly down into the heart of a text, like a bee in a flower, it is like heaven upon earth; it is as if the soul were bathing itself in morning dews; the dust and fret are washed off, and the noises recede into the distance; peace comes; we move aloft in another world—the world of ideas and realities; the mind mounts joyfully from one height to another; it sees the common world far beneath, yet clearly, in its true meaning and size and relations to other worlds. And then one comes down on Sabbath, to speak to the people, calm, strong, and clear, like Moses from the mount, and with a true Divine message.

"Lose your inner life, and you lose yourself, sure enough; for that is yourself. We take it for granted that you are a regenerated man, or we would not have ordained you to be a minister of the Gospel today. But it is possible for a man to be regenerate and to be a minister, and yet to remain worldly, shallow, undeveloped and unsanctified. We who are your brethren in the ministry could tell sad histories in illustration of this out of our own inner life. We could tell you how, in keeping the vineyard of others, we have often neglected our own; and how now, at the end of years of ministerial activity and incessant toil, we turn round and look with dismay at our shallow characters, our un-enriched minds, and our lack of spirituality and Christ-likeness. O brother! Take heed to thyself!"[13]

Chapter Two

Choosing the Scripture

An old recipe for a rabbit dish starts out, "First catch the rabbit." That puts first things first. Without the rabbit there is no dish.[14] Preachers often forget as they spend hours preparing a sermon, that the most important and powerful tool they have is the Bible. God may bless our homiletical outline, our illustrations and stories, our delivery, etc., but He does not promise to do so. He only promises to bless His Word, "For as the rain cometh down, and the snow from heaven, and returneth not thither, but watereth the earth, and maketh it bring forth and bud, that it may give seed to the sower, and bread to the eater: So shall my word be that goeth forth out of my mouth: it shall not return unto me void, but it shall accomplish that which I please, and it shall prosper in the thing whereto I sent it." (Isaiah 55:10-11) Consider what the prophet Jeremiah suggested, "The prophet that hath a dream, let him tell a dream; and he that hath my word, let him speak my word faithfully. What is the chaff to the wheat? saith the Lord. Is not my word like as a fire? saith the Lord; and like a hammer that breaketh the rock in pieces?" (Jeremiah 23:28-29)

Often preachers give the impression that the reading of Scripture is just a good way to get things started and nothing more. The Scripture reading has about as much to do with the sermon as the National Anthem has to do with a football game—it gets things started but is never heard from again! We must never forget that we are not called to stand in the pulpit and preach ourselves, our philosophy, our experiences, or even our beliefs. We are commanded to "preach the Word!"

Sermon Starters

Develop A Homiletical Mind

The second sermon I ever preached was to a group of teenagers at the Woodcrest Baptist Church in Minneapolis during my summer internship. I preached on the life of Judas Iscariot and entitled it "Thirty Pieces of Silver." I had worked hard in preparing that sermon and did my best to deliver it in the power of the Holy Spirit. God blessed and used it. After the teens had all filed out, the pastor's wife came over to me and thanked me for the message. I thanked her and said, "Mrs. Poorman, that's the only sermon I have. I don't know where your husband gets all of his sermons." I will never forget what she did. Looking straight into my eyes and holding the Bible up in front of her, she said, "This Book is filled with them!" From that moment on, every time I read a Bible truth, heard the Bible preached, or saw an illustration in life of a Bible principle, I would think about how that truth could be preached.

Spurgeon speaks of this in his lecture on "The Choice of a Text." He obviously had no time for lazy, unprepared preachers. "We should constantly preserve the holy activity of our minds. Woe unto the minister who dares to waste an hour… . A man who goes up and down from Monday morning till Saturday night, and indolently dreams that he is to have his text sent down by an angelic messenger in the last hour or two of the week, tempts God, and deserves to stand speechless on the Sabbath. We have no leisure as ministers; we are never off duty, but are on our watchtowers day and night… . The leaf of your ministry will soon wither unless, like the blessed man in the first Psalm, you meditate in the law of the Lord both day and night. I am most anxious that you should not throw away time in religious dissipation, or in gossiping and frivolous talk. Beware of running about from this meeting to that, listening to mere twaddle, and contributing your share to the general blowing up of windbags. A man great at tea-drinkings, evening parties, and Sunday school excursions, is generally little everywhere else. Your pulpit preparations are your first business, and if you neglect these, you will bring no credit upon yourself or your office.

"Ministers should always be making their hay, but especially when the sun shines. Thomas Spencer wrote, 'I keep a little book, in which I enter every text of Scripture which comes into my mind with power and sweetness. Were

I to dream of a passage of Scripture I should enter it, and when I sit down to compose I look over the book, and have never found myself at a loss for a subject.' Watch for your subjects as you go about the city or the country. Always keep your eyes and ears open, and you will hear and see angels. The world is full of sermons—catch them on the wing. A sculptor believes, whenever he sees a rough block of marble, that there is a noble statue concealed within it, and that he has only to chip away the superfluities and reveal it. So do you believe that there is within the husk of everything the kernel of a sermon for the wise man.... . Always a preacher be thou, O man of God, foraging for the pulpit, in all provinces of nature and art, storing and preparing at all hours and all seasons."[15]

Selecting A Text
The term "text" is derived from the Latin "textus," which in turn came from the verb "texere" meaning "to weave," "to construct," or "to compose." "Textus" is the product of the weaving, texture, web, structure. Text is thus the fabric of one's thinking expressed orally or in writing. As applied to preaching, the text was formally regarded as the scriptural fabric of the sermon into which were woven the comments and interpretations of the preacher. As preaching developed, the text became shorter, and the comments and interpretation became longer until the text became simply a scriptural starting point or foundation of the sermon. Correctly defined, the text is a complete unit of biblical thought which serves as the scriptural fabric or structure of the sermon.[16]

Expository preaching is more a philosophy than it is a method. The effective preacher will make Scripture the

Chapter Two - Choosing the Scripture 21

foundation of his message. Perry states, "If the sermonizer is directed to a passage of Scripture, then study of its content and context should guide him to a subject which will be both the subject of the passage and the subject of his sermon. If the "sermon starter" came from a source outside the Bible, the sermonizer will then go to the Scriptures to determine the location and extent of coverage given to this idea within the context of Scripture."[17]

The text may find the preacher or the preacher may find the text. Often as a preacher is reading the Scriptures, a passage will grip his own heart and become the basis for a sermon. Spurgeon states, "When a verse gives your mind a hearty grip, from which you cannot release yourself, you will need no further direction as to your proper theme. Like the fish, you nibble at many baits, but when the hook has fairly pierced you, you will wander no more. When the text gets a hold of us, we may be sure that we have a hold of it, and may safely deliver our souls upon it."[18]

Often, however, the idea for a sermon will come to the preacher based on the need of his audience. This is illustrated by the children of Issachar, "… which were men that had understanding of the times… ." (I Chronicles 12:32) The preacher must know his people as a shepherd knows his sheep. The needs that he sees will direct him to passages of Scripture that deal with that area. A pastor invited me to preach a three-day meeting on the subject of soulwinning which I was happy to do. He promoted the meeting as such and I prepared to preach messages on that theme. We had about forty-five minutes in the car from the airport to the church; and as we drove, he began to tell me how that just in the past few weeks an opportunity had come up for the church to relocate. They had outgrown their facility and this opportunity would afford them to grow their ministries significantly. He explained how it would be a huge step for the church to sell its existing property and move to a new site. I could tell he was deeply burdened that this move was the will of God and wanted his people to follow his leadership. By the time we got to the church, I said, "Pastor, I have a message on "faith" that I think would really help your people in this situation. I know you want me to preach on soulwinning, but would you allow me to pray about bringing that message on faith?" By the closing service we both felt liberty that I should preach on faith from the life of Jonathan and his armourbearer in I Samuel 13 and 14. God blessed the service and used it to encourage the people to trust God by faith. The message was motivated by the need and the Scripture was found to meet that need.

The text should always be a complete unit of thought. Be careful not to simply take a word, thought, phrase or clause out of its context to build your message. The shorter the text, the more danger there is in misinterpretation. Don't be afraid of familiar texts. "Familiar texts are the jewels of the pulpit—diamonds are never obsolete"—just ask your wife! If you are preaching to the same congregation each week, you should vary your texts as God commands us to preach the whole counsel of God (Acts 20:27).

Reading The Text

When you read your text in the pulpit, it should not be the first time you have read it out loud. The Bible is God speaking to man. We cannot improve on "thus saith the Lord." How sad it is that we hurriedly and clumsily read through our Scripture, getting it out of the way, so that we

Chapter Two - Choosing the Scripture

can spend the next thirty minutes preaching our sermon. We might be more effective if we properly read the Bible for thirty minutes, made a few comments and gave the invitation. Have you ever been misquoted or misinterpreted? How did you feel? How must God feel when we mispronounce words in the Bible, read with no voice inflection or meaning, and never pause at proper points of punctuation, so that the meaning will be felt by the listener?

Preacher, there is absolutely nothing in your sermon—no illustration, no quotation, no poem, no funny story, no explanation, no life experience, etc. that is more powerful than the pure Words of God Himself. We must read our Scripture as though it were the most important thing that the audience will hear in the sermon—because it is! Practice reading your text out loud several times. Stand in your pulpit as you do. Use a conversational tone, voice inflections, and a variety of rate. Your goal in reading the Scripture should be to transport your audience into the setting of your text.

I had a professor in college who had previously been a pastor in Buffalo, New York. He told of a time that he desired to preach on a busy street corner in downtown Buffalo but wasn't sure how he could draw a crowd together. He placed his top hat on the sidewalk with his Bible concealed underneath it and began to shout, "It's Alive!" "It's Alive!" Soon a crowd gathered around him at which time he picked up his hat, held up the Bible and declared its "living" contents. Often today we declare to our audience by the way we read the Scripture, "It's Dead! It's Lifeless! It has no power to change your life!" No wonder the average Christian never reads his Bible or is out in some bookstore looking for some watered down version that he thinks will help him get something. We have convinced him that our Bible from which we read has nothing to offer him.

Two atheists were conversing in Chicago years ago. The one told his friend that he was going to go and hear D.L. Moody preach. The other responded with, "Surely you don't believe what he preaches do you?" The first answered, "No, but he sure does!" If anyone ought to believe the Bible it ought to be the one preaching it! Read your text like you believe it!

Approaching The Text
As we approach a text, we must come to it in three ways. First, we must come with a submissive approach. We must not come with a preconceived notion or understanding. We must bend our thoughts to the Scriptures, not the Scriptures to our thoughts. Too often, we form our beliefs and then try to find a verse to prove ourselves right. We will never change the Bible to fit our lives. We must change our lives to fit the Bible.

Secondly, we must come with a simple approach. Let the Scripture say what it means—do not try to read into it what is not there. Read to understand, then experience what you understand. The Bible is not complex—God wrote it to be understood. Monroe Parker was once preaching a meeting where he knew that a large number of pastors would be in attendance. As a result, he worked diligently on a message that would be at their level. He went to the pulpit that night completely satisfied with his deep theological message that would surely impress the other ministers in attendance. However, as he glanced over the crowd during the song service, he noticed a good number of lost people also in attendance. He knew the message he had prepared was way over their heads, but he tried to ignore the thought of changing his message. The last congregational hymn was announced and he began to sing the words to "Christ Receiveth Sinful Men." The words of the chorus pierced his soul—"make the message clear and plain, Christ receiveth sinful men." He tucked his well prepared outline into the back of his Bible, took out a pen and scratched out a few simple notes, and stood moments later and preached the Gospel from John 3:16. Many were saved! No doubt someone along the way has asked you to use the "KISS" approach in preaching—that is Keep It Short, Stupid!" May I amend that just slightly and say, "Keep It Simple, Stupid!"

Lastly, we must come with a studious approach. Not all of God's truths are found on the surface—we must dig for them. "If thou seekest her as silver, and searchest for her as for hid treasures; Then thou shalt understand the fear of the Lord, and find the knowledge of God." (Proverbs 2: 4-5) "Study to shew thyself approved unto God, a workman that needeth not to be ashamed, rightly dividing the word of truth." (II Timothy 2:15) Never apologize for time spent in studying the Scriptures.

Discovering The Basic Meaning Of The Text

We will cover this in more detail in succeeding chapters, but as we choose our text, we must at least look for the central theme of the passage. Be careful not to just uncover the meaning of words. Word studies can be fun and certainly reveal the rich depth of Scripture, but the meaning of a word is not as important as what is being communicated through the use of those words. Simply knowing the meaning of words is as pointless as reading the dictionary! Words are linked together to convey meaning. I doubt seriously that any young man has ever gotten out a dictionary while reading a love letter from his girl friend. He desires to find the overall message rather than the meaning of some word. The Bible is God's letter to us and although an understanding of His specific Words is valuable—do not miss the overall message.

Look for what is being communicated in the passage. Communication is described as a "meeting of meanings." We must help our audience pull up a chair to the table where the biblical writers sat. We must understand their language, their culture, their background, etc. We must help our audience focus on what the Bible is saying to the original listener and then see how that applies to us today.

Let The Text Speak To You
God always deals with the preacher first. As stated earlier, the man affects the message. If the man is not affected by the message, the message will have no affect. Haddon W. Robinson quotes a number of men in making this point. "The truth must be applied to the personality and experience of the preacher. This places God's dealing with the preacher at the center of the process. As much as we might wish otherwise, the preacher cannot be separated from the message.... Phillips Brooks was on to something when he described preaching as 'truth poured through personality.' The man affects his message. He may be mouthing a scriptural idea yet remain as impersonal as a telephone recording, as superficial as a radio commercial, or as manipulative as a 'con' man. The audience does not hear a sermon, they hear a man. Bishop William A. Quayle had this in mind when he rejected standard definitions of

homiletics. 'Preaching is the art of making a sermon and delivering it?' he asked. 'Why no, that is not preaching. Preaching is the art of making a preacher and delivering that!' Expository preaching should develop the preacher into a mature Christian. As the expositor studies the Bible, the Holy Spirit studies him. When a man prepares expository sermons, God prepares the man. As P.T. Forsyth said, 'The Bible is the supreme preacher to the preacher.'"[19]

Before a man proclaims the message of the Bible to others, he should live with that message himself. God is more interested in developing "messengers" than He is "messages." A preacher must learn to listen to God before he speaks for Him.

Applying The Text To The Audience
Application is what gives the preaching purpose. Preaching is boring when there is no application to life. People are concerned with gas prices, the job market, their quarrel with their girl friend, diagnosis of cancer—a rat race that only rats seem to ever win. If the sermon does not make a difference in that world, they wonder if it makes any difference at all.

Several years ago while I was conducting a revival meeting, I sat in an adult Sunday school class that was taught by a layman. He was teaching a series of lessons through the "feasts" of the Old Testament. I was fascinated by his knowledge of the Bible with respect to these feasts. Frankly, I had never personally paid much attention to them, and I listened carefully as he explained their significance to the people of the Old Testament. As the time wound down, I kept thinking, "How is he going to apply this to our lives today?" I couldn't wait for him to give the application, but it never came. I remember going away from that class totally frustrated with knowledge that had no impact on my life.

The audience does not come to church to convict Judas, or Peter, or Solomon, but to judge themselves. Paul's sermons and letters were delivered to specific Christians with specific needs. The preacher must know his message, but he must also know how that message applies to his audience. "May God apply this to our lives" at the close of the sermon just won't cut it in this day of intense problems.

The challenge is obvious. We must preach the Word if we are to impact lives. The text we choose must become the fabric of the sermon. If indeed, what God says is the most important thing in our sermon, we must choose the text carefully, study it continually, read it with conviction, and preach it with compassion.

F.B. Meyer understood the awe with which a biblical preacher speaks to the issues of his age, "He is in a line of great succession. The Reformers, the Puritans, the Pastors of the Pilgrim fathers were all essentially expositors. They did not announce their own particular opinions, which might be a matter of private interpretation or doubtful disposition, but taking their stand on the Scripture, drove home their message with irresistible effect with 'Thus saith the Lord.'"[20]

Henry Ward Beecher in his lecture, "The Preacher's Book," states, "First of all things, be ye transformed into spiritual Bible-men. If you had not another volume on earth, you could make very excellent preachers of yourselves by the Word of the Lord. Allow me to speak of my own early ministry in this respect. I owe more to the Book of Acts and to the writings of the Apostle Paul than to all other books put together. I was sent into the wilderness of Indiana to preach among the poor and ignorant, and I lived much in my saddle. My library was in my saddle-bags; I went from camp-meeting to camp-meeting and from log-hut to log-hut. I had my New Testament, and from it I learned that which has been the very secret of any success that I have had in the Christian ministry. My strength has been in the love of Christ; in the glory of that conception of God which is in Christ Jesus; in the sense that my business was to win men; and in my attempt to win them by bringing the same influences to bear upon them which I found abounding throughout the New Testament. Blessed it would be, for many of you, if you could be shut up to the Bible in your work, if, for several years, at least during the earlier part of your ministry, you could go into the field, taking your Bible in your hand, and with it labor for men, for their conversion and for their salvation."[21]

Chapter Three

Collecting the Facts

Have you ever had a great seed thought for a sermon only to be totally frustrated later when there just did not seem to be enough material to make a sermon out of it? I always keep a blank sheet of paper in the front of my Bible so that when one of these "seeds" for a sermon hits me, I can jot it down. I have a whole file of those thoughts that have never quite made it to sermon status. I have preached some of my best sermons in my dreams while I slept. (Thousands of decisions have been made too!) In the morning, I could remember the text and some of the points, but for the life of me I have never been able to construct a sermon out of those "dream" sermons.

When God calls us to preach, He puts within us an intense desire to proclaim His Word. Paul states it well in I Corinthians 9:16: "...for necessity is laid upon me; yea, woe is unto me, if I preach not the gospel!" Jeremiah states in chapter twenty and verse nine: "... But his word was in mine heart as a burning fire shut up in my bones, and I was weary with forbearing, and I could not stay." When once the message of God's Word has gripped our hearts, the delivery of that message comes easy—we have to get it out!

Putting that message on paper, however, can be tedious and time consuming. Like the athlete who realizes that games are won in the off-season weight room when no one is watching, so the preacher realizes that the effectiveness of the sermon will be determined by the hours in his study as he labors to properly build his message.

Naturally, every preacher wants to immediately come up with a good outline, maybe even alliterated, within five minutes of settling on a text. Some portions of Scripture outline well and lend themselves to a homiletical style easily. But unfortunately, God didn't send down a "Preacher's Edition" of the Bible in outline form with illustrations for each point in the margin and questions to answer at the end of each chapter. Our responsibility, like the scribes of the Old Testament, is to read the Scriptures and then make sense of them so that the people can understand and obey them. "So they read in the book of the law of God distinctly, and gave the sense, and caused them to understand the reading." (Nehemiah 8:8)

But before we start on an outline, it will be well worth our time to get out a clean sheet of paper and with the Bible text before us, collect some facts about the passage. Don't worry about what your page looks like or if it has any logical order to it—just jot down everything that comes to your mind from the passage. The "seed" in your mind must be nurtured into a full sermon by the collecting of material from the passage itself, other passages, your own experience, or someone else's thoughts and ideas. Remember, "think homiletically." How is this going to apply? What is the problem to be solved, the principle to be lived, etc. that will make the Scriptures come alive to your audience? A sermon always involves exposition as well as application.

As you read and re-read the text and meditate on its message, let me offer some questions to answer on your sheet of paper in front of you:

1. What group of Bible books are you in? If you are in Ephesians, you may want to study the background of the four books that make up the "Prison Epistles."
2. What is the background of the particular book you are in?
3. What is the central theme of the book?
4. What is the background of the human author of the book?
5. Where was the book written?
6. When was it written?
7. To whom was it written?
8. What prompted the writing of this book?
9. Are there any repeated or peculiar terms in the passage?
10. What is the general tone of the passage? Argumentative? Exhortative? Instructive?
11. What is the general application of the message in the text?

12. What is the dominant impression you get as you read the passage?
13. Who are the major and minor people in the text?
14. Are there repeated words or phrases in the passage?
15. Does a distinctive name or title fit this passage as a means of identification?
16. Is there an obvious outline in the passage?
17. Are there significant breaks in the passage between thoughts?
18. Are there several key ideas or points in the passage?
19. What are some parallel passages of Scripture to this one if any? Remember, the best commentary on the Bible is the Bible.
20. Is there additional information in the parallel passages that sheds any light on the text?
21. What is the grammatical style?
22. What clues does the punctuation give with respect to declarations, exclamations, or questions?
23. Is there any meaning or background to words in the passage that will give color and illustration to the passage?
24. Do the verb tenses give indication of meaning? Remember, Greek verb tenses can be more specific than they are in English.
25. Does the word order in the sentences give any indication to meaning? In the Greek, the most important words always come first.
26. Are there any figures of speech that can be used for clarification or illustration?

Chapter Three - Collecting the Facts

27. Are there repeated, peculiar, or distinctive terms that may provide a basis for your sermon points?
28. Is there an interrogative adverb in the passage? Who, What, When, Where, or How.
29. Is there a personal, community, or national problem cited directly or indirectly?
30. Is there an answer, cure, or solution to a problem found in the passage?
31. Does the text divide into paragraphs and if so, are there key points in each paragraph?
32. Is there a Bible character in the passage and if so, why is he or she mentioned?
33. Are there any familiar verses in the passage?
34. Are there "cause and effect" relationships in the text?
35. Is there any specific doctrine in the passage?
36. Is there a specific activity mentioned that should be practiced or avoided?
37. How does the passage affect lives practically?
38. Do any personal life experiences come to mind that are relative to this text?
39. Do any other illustrations come to mind?
40. Do any quotations, poems, statistics, etc. come to mind that would provide additional material?

Answering these questions will provide a "ton" of material from which to construct your sermon. Don't try to be too "homiletical" at this early stage of "collecting the facts." Just put down every idea, thought, Scripture, illustration, quotation, etc. that comes to your mind on your scratch sheet of paper. Don't worry about where it might fit or if it will fit at all. You are just gathering ideas.

The more sermons you prepare, the more this process of thinking "homiletically" will come naturally. You won't be able to write fast enough!

Chapter Four
Constructing the Introduction

How are we going to get from reading our text to points one, two, three, etc.? The greatest sermon in the world will be a flop if the foundation for preaching is not properly and effectively laid. If no one is listening, what good is our homiletical outline?

The introduction to the message is crucial for two reasons. First, it must capture the attention of the audience. We must engage their interest and give them a reason to listen. They must sense from the very start that this is going to help—I need this! Secondly, the introduction must lay the groundwork for what is ahead. It is a foundation for what is going to be built later. It must establish the purpose for the message, so that the audience can be prepared to respond.

"When a minister steps behind the pulpit, he dare not assume that his congregation sits expectantly on the edge of the pews waiting for his sermon. In reality they are probably a bit bored and harbor a suspicion that he will make matters worse. A Russian proverb offers wise counsel to the preacher: 'It is the same with men as with donkeys: whoever would hold them fast must get a very good grip on their ears!' The opening words of a sermon therefore need not be dramatic; they need not even be plain; but they must go after the minds of the hearers to force them to listen. If the preacher does not capture attention in the first thirty seconds, he may never gain it at all."[22]

"The purpose of the introduction is to lead the congregation into the matter to be discussed. If it fails to do that, it fails. The preacher has been studying the passage of Scripture from which he will preach, and thinking about it for some time... the congregation has not. They come to the passage cold; that is why an introduction is in order.... Orienting a congregation involves arresting attention and creating interest. Arresting, or getting attention, is absolutely essential; until you have done so, the congregation will hear nothing that you will have to say, no matter how valuable or interesting it may be. But on the other hand, once you have gained a hearing, you must hold it. That is done by creating interest. It is of little value to gain attention if that is not immediately turned into interest. The function of a good introduction is to do both."[23]

The length of the introduction will vary with the material of the message and to some degree the length of

Chapter Four - Constructing the Introduction

the entire message. There can be a danger in being too long and thus taking away from the main body of the sermon, or being too short and thus not allowing the listener enough time to focus in his mind on the subject matter. Some messages will need more of an introduction because of the background material that is necessary to set the stage for the message. Other messages can be introduced in a few simple statements and an illustration.

We will cover illustrations in chapter six, but in most sermons you will need at least one in your introduction. Personally, I have found that a good illustration given immediately after the Scripture reading arrests the attention of the audience and draws them into the subject matter before their minds have a chance to wander to something else. This is especially true when preaching to lost people or carnal Christians who may not be there for the sole purpose of getting something from the sermon. I was preaching one evening in a revival meeting on the rapture. To illustrate in the introduction how quickly this event could take place, I kicked my feet out behind me and fell face down to the floor, right in the middle of a sentence. After picking myself up (realizing thankfully that I had not hurt myself in the process), I said, "Faster than it took me to fall to the floor, the rapture could take place and Christians would be gone!" A young man in his early twenties was saved that night at the close. When he returned the following night, he said, "Sir, when you hit that floor—you had my attention."

But putting the illustration aside for a moment, let's look at the three basic parts to a solid and effective introduction or foundation to the sermon.

The Declaration

Determining The Subject Of The Text

The subject should come from the core of the passage of Scripture that you have selected for a text. This is the central theme upon which you are going to build the message. This central idea of the text may be:

>A doctrine to proclaim.
>A duty to perform.
>A principle to live.
>A problem to solve.
>A calling to pursue.

This subject of the text becomes the subject of your sermon. Subjects for sermons are often one word or a short phrase. Be careful not to make the subject too broad in scope that the message misses the specific emphasis of the passage. For example, "prayer" is a worthy subject for a sermon, but if the passage deals with a certain type of prayer, such as intercessory prayer, then this should be the subject.

Surveying The Subject

Hopefully, you still have your scratch sheet in front of you. But in case you skipped that step, here are a few questions you ought to ask yourself with respect to this subject matter in the text:

1. What have I read on this subject?
2. What have I observed in my experience which may throw light on the subject?
3. What does the Bible say in other places on this subject?
4. Do I have any personal bias or attitude on this subject?

5. Does the audience to whom I will be preaching have any bias or attitude on this subject?
6. Are there any famous quotations, poems, or illustrations that I can immediately recall on this subject?
7. Is the subject current or relative to a present situation?

Formulating the Declaration Statement

The first essential ingredient in our introduction is a strong declaration statement. We will simply refer to it as our "Declaration." This statement simply and clearly states the specific subject matter of the text and allows the audience to know what the sermon is going to be about. Notice in the following examples how we take the subject matter and turn it into a Declaration Statement:

Subject	*Declaration Statement*
Prayer	There is great profit in prayer.
The Church	God wants every Christian to actively serve in the church.
Soulwinning	Every Christian is commanded to be a soulwinner.
Discouragement	God does not intend for any of us to live in discouragement.
Hell	Hell is a literal and awful place.
The Home	The home is God's first and foremost institution.
The Truth	God's truth is available and knowable to all of us.

This statement should always be declarative or exclamatory in nature. It becomes the basis for the message and begins to let the audience know where we are going in the sermon. Avoid long compound sentences—keep it simple—your outline will enable you to expand this truth later.

The Proposition

What Is A Proposition?
Books on preaching will call this ingredient by different names. Some refer to this as the "central idea." Others call it the "purpose statement" while others refer to it as the "thesis." I like to call it the "proposition" because in it we are going to propose to the audience what they need to do with the subject matter of the text before us.

The Proposition Is The Key To The Introduction
In reality, this is where the "application" of the message begins. What you state here will be the same thing that you will ask them to respond to at the close of the sermon. The proposition ties the entire sermon together in its application of the subject matter to the listener. It becomes the "steering wheel" of the sermon. It will keep you as the preacher on track and it will keep the audience focused on the subject matter and how it relates to them. This proposition is what ties the Bible truth to the present. Good preaching is always in the present tense. It must speak to the concerns of the day in the language of the present. It must be true to the impact of the Scripture and at the same time be relevant to human experiences.

In *Preaching with Purpose,* Jay Adams refers to this as the "Purpose" and suggests that preachers write that purpose on the top of each page of their notes so as not to lose sight of "why" they are preaching the message.

Framing the Proposition
Personally, I like to use a question in my proposition. For example in our sermon "The Truth" from James 1:16-27, our Declaration Statement listed above was: God's Truth is available and knowable to all of us. My proposition would be: Have you received God's truth, or are you being deceived? (By the way, both words—received and deceived are in the text and will be used in the outline later.) I like the question here because as someone has aptly said, "Statements, accuse—Questions, convict." For example, the statement, "You're on your way to Hell!" is certainly true for the lost person, but is received as an accusation. The average person in the audience immediately puts up a defense mechanism and says, "Who does he think he is? Doesn't he know that I go to church? I'm as good a person as half the people in here, etc." They are immediately turned off by your statement. But let's word the same truth as a question: "Have you ever thought about what it would be like to spend eternity in Hell?" You have immediately challenged the person in the pew to think. He must answer that question and if he cannot, he is inclined to listen to you explain to him how he can escape such a place. Isn't this what we do when we witness to people? Often, after breaking the ice, we will say, "Could I ask you a personal question?" If they give us permission, that question will probably be something like, "If you were to die today, are you 100 percent sure you would go to Heaven?" If the person does not know, the conviction has already begun.

The earlier in the sermon you can build conviction, the longer the Holy Spirit has to use that conviction to bring about a decision. Remember, He is the One who has to draw them, so give Him ample time to do so. Application of the truth should not be saved for the conclusion, but begin immediately in the introduction. The question that you pose in the proposition can be answered in the points of your outline. (More on that later.)

The proposition can be repeated often throughout the sermon. Varying its form will be helpful. In the proposition we may ask, "Have you received the truth of God's Word or are you being deceived?" Later we may ask: "Are you rejecting God's truth today?" "Has Satan deceived you into believing a lie?" "Are you sure that you have embraced the truth?" Keeping the proposition before the audience throughout the sermon enables the conviction of the Holy Spirit to build.

The Transitional Sentence

Building A Bridge

The transitional sentence is a verbal bridge that will take us from the introduction to the body of the sermon. The platform or foundation has been set: We have declared the subject matter. We have started the application process with a convicting question in our proposition. Now we must smoothly make a transition to the outline. This transitional sentence will take the information that has preceded it and make a logical transition to that which is to follow.

The body of the sermon, or outline, is going to answer some of the questions for the listener from the subject matter. For example: Why do I need to receive God's truth?

Chapter Four - Constructing the Introduction | 45

What benefits are there in the truth of God's Word? How is this truth available to me? What will happen if I reject the truth of God? You have raised the question, the Holy Spirit is using it to build conviction in the heart, now answer it!

The transitional sentence must have a "key word." This key word labels your points in your outline so that you don't have to call them "point one," "point two," etc. Usually a modifier or two in front of this key word in the transitional sentence will magnify it to the audience. For example: "Today we are going to see four vitally important CHARACTERS in the arena of truth." The key word is "characters" with "vitally" and "important" as the modifiers given for emphasis. Now instead of having to say, "The first "thing" or my first "point," we can say as we introduce the first point in the outline, "Our first "character" in the arena of truth is…"

Here are some examples of key words that can be used: Arguments, Benefits, Blessings, Commands, Dangers, Effects, Gains, Guarantees, Honors, Imperatives, Improvements, Incentives, Invitations, Issues, Joys, Judgments, Lessons, Losses, Needs, Obligations, Orders, Penalties, Predictions, Privileges, Profits, Reasons, Results, Rewards, Satisfactions, Steps, Values, Blunders, Excesses, Extremes, Mistakes, Instructions, Guidelines, Patterns, Plans, Practices, Prescriptions, Rules, Stipulations, Admonitions, Commands, Laws, Fears, Precautions, Sayings, Preparations, Provisions, Details, Directives, Injunctions, Teachings, Barriers, Fundamentals, Obstacles, Powers, Means, Alternatives, Systems, … The list is endless—use your imagination!

My homiletics instructor made it emphatically clear that we must never use the word "THINGS" as our key word. He would tease us by asking, "What is a thing? There has to be a more descriptive word than THINGS!" We laughed, but he was serious. He informed us that if we used the word THINGS as our key word in that class we would automatically fail! It came time for our final exam which consisted of standing before the class and preaching a short message. I will never forget a young man by the name of Robin who stood to preach. He sailed through his Scripture reading, his declaration and proposition. And then he did it—He said, "Today I would like you to notice with me three THINGS…" Immediately out of the corner of my eye, I saw my five-foot tall, one hundred pound professor, Dr. Richard Weeks, stand to his feet, and with every ounce of energy in his little body and with veins sticking out of his neck, he exclaimed: "Robin, sit down! You have flunked this course!"

I have never forgotten the soberness of that moment and although Dr. Weeks has been in Heaven for a number of years, I am always afraid that he may be listening. As far as I can recall, I have never used the word THINGS in my transitional sentence. May I encourage you to be a little more creative as well?

Putting It All Together
Suppose that you have selected James 1:16-27 as your text. Perhaps on your scratch paper you have put the following:

> *Text:* James 1:16-27
> *Subject:* Truth
> *Proposition:* Do we know truth?

Chapter Four - Constructing the Introduction | 47

Transitional Sentence: Four characters in the passage.

Formalizing these "seeds" into an Introduction that's ready for preaching is now necessary.

> *Title:* "What is Truth?
> *Text:* James 1:16-27
> *Declaration:* God's truth is available and knowable to each of us!
> *Proposition:* Have you received the truth of God or are you being deceived?
> *Transitional Sentence:* Notice with me four vitally important CHARACTERS in the arena of truth.

There you have it—a basic skeleton of the key components necessary for an effective introduction. Granted, you may have an illustration or two somewhere in there, some additional Scripture verses either from the text or another parallel passage that will give weight to the subject matter, or perhaps a quotation, etc., but you have now determined exactly where you are going in the sermon. By the way, your audience also knows. What you will ask them to do in the conclusion will be no surprise!

With this foundation in place—the rest is a piece of cake!

When I finish teaching the introduction in our Homiletics class in the college, we stop and let each of the young men prepare and preach an introduction. They have only five minutes to present it and they are not allowed to give anything beyond the introduction. It is amazing the conviction in the room as one after another, these young men stand and follow this plan. On a number of occasions, by the end of the class, someone blurts out, "Whew! Give the invitation!"

There are three types of preachers: those to whom you "cannot" listen; those to whom you "can" listen; and those to whom you "must" listen. During the introduction the congregation usually decides what kind of speaker is addressing them that day.[24]

CHAPTER FIVE

Creating an Outline

When someone hires an architect to design a building, that architect upon accepting the job, will ask two important questions? What is this building going to be used for? And, what do you want it to look like? As the architect designs that building, he begins with a concept that is derived from "function," that is, what the building is to do and "form," that is, what it is supposed to look like. A bowling alley has a different function than an office building and a church will look differently than a restaurant. Function and form are the guideposts in the mind of the architect.

At this point we know "what" we have to preach (the text) and "why" we are preaching it (the proposition).

Now we must determine "how" we are going to carry out this purpose. Two questions should be in the mind of the preacher as he sits down to write the sermon. What is this sermon going to look like—its "form" and how am I going to communicate the truth so as to achieve the desired results—its "function." A sermon to junior church children will have a different form than the one preached to a group of senior saints, but its function may be the same. A sermon at a funeral may have the same form as the sermon preached at a youth rally, but its function will be different.

For the building to be constructed, the architect must turn his idea into a blue-print showing in detail how the concept will translate into steel, stone, and glass. Likewise the preacher, having derived a concept from the text and the need of his audience, must now fashion a blue-print—the "outline" of the sermon. This blueprint will give the sermon a sense of order, unity, and purpose.

The Purposes Of An Outline

Four Main Reasons For An Outline
Some preachers are what we call "manuscript preachers" in that they write out every word of their sermon and become adept at reading it in the pulpit. Although I would not criticize this approach, there are four basic reasons why an outline is preferred. First, it clarifies in the preacher's eye and mind the relationships between the parts of the sermon. At a quick glance he is able to see main points as opposed to sub-points and illustrations in contrast to parallel Scripture passages. Second, it enables the preacher to view the sermon as a whole and intensifies the need for unity. From the press-box, a coach is able to see the entire playing field and

easily tell if his team is playing as a unit, whereas the coach on the sideline is only able to watch a part of his team. The outline shows the preacher the unity between all parts of the sermon. Third, an outline gives order to the sermon so that the listener will get the information in a logical sequence. The Word of God is in logical sequence according to Isaiah 28:10: "For precept must be upon precept; precept upon precept; line upon line, line upon line; here a little, and there a little." The outline allows for this same logical sequence in the sermon. Fourth, the outline helps the preacher see the places in the sermon that will need additional support and material. At a glance it is easy to detect where additional Scripture is needed, or an illustration would help, etc.

The Outline Should Be Flexible But Clearly Marked
Not every passage of Scripture will outline well, nor will every text have an equal number of points. These points will not always have an equal value—some will be more significant than others. The most fundamental ideas will become your main points and make up the structure around which the body of your sermon is built. These main points should be marked by Roman numerals. For example, in our message on "What is Truth," the four characters in the arena of truth would be identified as follows:

I. The Provider of Truth (James 1:17-20)

II. The Possessor of Truth (James 1:21)

III. The Pretender of Truth (James 1:22-24)

IV. The Performer of Truth (James 1:25-27)

The Sub-Points Of The Outline

Simply listing the main points does not develop the sermon. Main points need expansion, so secondary points are added. A capital letter designates these sub-points and they should be indented slightly. Continuing our sermon on truth:

I. The Provider of Truth (James 1:17-20)
   A. An Unparalleled Origin (verse 17)
   B. An Unbelievable Offer (verse 18)
   C. An Unwise Opposition (verses 19-20)

II. The Possessor of Truth (James 1:21)
   A. A Repentance from Sin (verse 21a)
   B. A Receiving of the Scriptures (verse 21b)

III. The Pretender of Truth (James 1:22-24)
   A. He Notices his Condition (verses 22-24a)
   B. He Neglects to Change (verse 24b)

IV. The Performer of Truth (James 1:25-27)
   A. A Bridled Speech (verse 25-26)
   B. A Benevolent Spirit (verse 27a)
   C. A Blameless Separation (verse 27b)

These sub-points improve the outline by making it clearer and more specific. With each expansion of the outline, the substance of the sermon becomes more obvious. A person who has never looked at the passage of Scripture should be able to look at your outline and have a good idea of what the sermon is about.

Stay As Basic As Possible

A sermon outline as opposed to a research paper outline should be simple and clear and have relatively few points.

Too many sub-points will confuse the listener. The capacity to remember is limited to a few points. The maturity of your audience will determine this to some degree.

In your main points, statements are better than questions. Your proposition has raised the question—now your main points should answer it. Work on some linking sentences to tie your main points together. Avoid saying, "Point number one is," or "my second point is." Each new point should logically progress from the previous one. Sometimes the previous idea and the new idea can be stated in the linking sentence. For example between points two and three in the above example, we could say, "Not only does the Bible show us who the "possessor of truth" is, but also warns us that some are merely "pretenders of truth."

Making The Outline Come Alive

The outline is merely the skeleton. Outlines are to sermons what skeletons are to the human body. In most sermons, as in most human bodies, the skeleton is not completely hidden, but we don't want too much of it to show. The bare bones of the body are covered with flesh. Supporting material is to the sermon what skin is to the body and what walls are to the frame of the house.

The audience will not respond to mere points or ideas. No one is ever moved to a decision by reading an outline. As the sermon is delivered, the listener will ask questions in his mind like, "I wonder what he means by that?" or "What evidence does he have for making that statement?" or "Sounds impressive, but how will that work in my life?" Thus we must now clarify, amplify, prove, and apply the ideas from Scripture and make them understandable, appealing, and worthy of a response.

Types Of Support Materials

Restatement

Restatement uses the principle of stating something "in other words." This allows the truth declared to gain clarity. Listeners must get what we say when we say it—they can't go back and hear it again—there is no "instant replay." This is where listening to preaching is different than reading a book. By restating the truth we are giving the audience a second chance to grasp it. In the following example we can see how Clovis G. Chappell uses restatement in his introduction to a sermon on the woman taken in adultery:

"The scholars are uncertain as to where in the sacred roll this story belongs. Some think that it does not belong at all. From certain ancient manuscripts it is omitted. However, speaking not as a scholar, but merely as a Bible reader, I am sure that it does really belong. Here I feel is a true story. If it is not true, it is one from which the truth itself might learn. Not only is this story true, but in my judgment it is factual. It is the record of an event that actually took place. It would have taken a superb genius indeed to have invented a story so true to life. Certainly it is consistent with what we know about the Scribes and Pharisees; it is yet more consistent with what we know about Jesus Himself."[25]

Restatement also impresses truth upon the listener. When we say something once, it can be ignored, but when it is repeated several times, it is underlined in the listeners thoughts and feelings. The advertisement industry spends millions of dollars annually repeating their message over and over again, on radio, television, in newspaper ads, and on billboards. Peter Marshall drives truth home through restatement in a sermon entitled "The Art of Moving Mountains." "I am sure that each of you has read this statement many times: Prayer changes things. You have seen it painted on posters which adorn the walls of our Sunday school rooms You have seen it stamped on little metal plates, read it in the Bible, heard it from the pulpit, oh, so many times. But do you believe it? Do you actually, honestly, believe that prayer changes things? Have you ever had prayer change anything for you? Your attitudes, your circumstances, your fears, your obstacles?"[26]

Restatement is different than repetition. Repetition is saying the same thing in the same words, while restatement is saying the same thing in different words. The skillful preacher will learn to restate a point several times in different ways.

Explanation And Definition
For many Bible terms and ideas to be understood, they must be defined and explained. A definition sets down what is included or excluded by a term or statement—it puts limits on the ideas that we are speaking of. Explanation shows how these ideas are related to each other—how they are similar or different from each other. Often through comparison and contrast people are able to grasp what the Bible means. Ray C. Stedman does this when he asks in a sermon:

"What do we mean when we say a thing is holy?" He answers, "Look at your Bible and it says, 'Holy Bible.' What makes it holy? The land of Israel is called the 'Holy Land' and the city of Jerusalem is called 'The Holy City.' Why? There is a quality about all three which they share in common. They all belong to God. The Bible is God's Book; Israel is God's land; Jerusalem is God's city—they are God's property! That is why they are holy; they belong to God!"[27]

I think you can see how you could take the above explanation of the word "holy" and make an application to the Christian's life. Why are we to be holy? Because we also belong to God!

It is important that as preachers we are aware of the maturity of our audience. It is always better to define too many terms rather than too few. Oftentimes, the more that we are familiar with a subject, the less we may be aware of our audience's ignorance. I'm confident that most of you that are reading this book could quote John 3:16 in your sleep, but do you realize there are people that have never once heard that verse? I was preaching in Connecticut in a young church that was meeting in a community center. That afternoon I had met a Roman Catholic priest and I invited him to come to the service that night. My son and I were standing in the back of the building about a half hour before the service straightening out some preaching tapes of mine on the back table. Suddenly, I looked up, and this Catholic priest was standing beside me. He picked up one of the tapes from the table entitled *John 3:16*. He asked, "What's this about?" I said, "Well, it is a simple Gospel message from that verse in the Bible." He said, "What does the verse say?" I opened my Bible and read it to him. He said, "Wow, that's quite a verse!" He had never once seen it! The longer we live in this post-Christian era in America, the more explaining of the Bible we are going to be doing.

Be sure you understand what you are speaking about. If a biblical truth is unclear in your mind, you will not come across clearly to your audience. A "mist" in the pulpit will become "fog" in the pew!

Factual Information
Facts consist of observations, examples, statistics, and other data that may be verified by the audience. Remember, we are living in the "information age" and people have access by way of the Internet to the "facts" you state—they can check it out to make sure you are telling the truth. A lost person will figure that if you lie about a fact to embellish some truth you are presenting, you are probably also lying about the Gospel that will save him from his sin. If you are presenting Bible facts, the listener should be able to look in the Bible and verify the truth of what you are saying. "These were more noble than those in Thessalonica, in that they received the word with all readiness of mind, and searched the scriptures daily, whether those things were so." (Acts 17:11)

Be careful that when you state something as fact that it is not just a matter of opinion. The preacher may say, "As a matter of fact, the greatest threat to the Christian home is working moms." This is more a matter of opinion than fact. Every man has a right to his opinion, but nobody has a right to be wrong about his facts! Solid, verifiable facts will add to the respect given to the messenger and the message.

Statistics can also be helpful in a number conscious culture. But again, be careful—you can make numbers say what you want them to. The classic example is: A report a number of years ago showed that thirty-three and a third percent of all co-eds at Johns Hopkins University had married faculty members. The percentage was accurate. Johns Hopkins had only three women students at the time and one of them had married a faculty member!

Keep you figures simple. Rounded off numbers can be used without sacrificing accuracy. A math major might be impressed that the population of Chicago in 1950 was 3,620,962, but most of us would find it easier to understand "a little over three and a half million people."

It also helps to compare statistical data with something that people already understand. Perhaps you have heard the principle of education which states that we must "take people from the 'known' to the 'unknown.'" That's the idea here. Compare the statistics of the concept you are trying to convey with something that they are already familiar with. For example: In describing the temple of Diana in Ephesus we might say, "It was 180 feet wide, over 375 feet long, with columns that towered sixty feet in height," and then add, "The temple was wider and longer than a football field including the end-zones, and the columns were taller than a five-story building."

Another example from Alan H. Monroe: "A speaker made understandable the small size of an electron by first giving the decimal fraction, which was incomprehensible and then added: If the electron were increased in size till it became as large as an apple, and a human being grew in the same proportion, that person could hold the entire solar system in the palm of his hand and would have to use a magnifying glass in order to see it."[28]

Quotations

When someone else has stated an idea better than we can, we use his words. Often this person we are quoting is in a better position to speak on the matter than we are or has a high credential that our audience will respect and accept.

Quotations should be used for two reasons—authority and impressiveness.

For example, every preacher believes in the doctrine of "Original Sin." However, I have run into a few folks along the way who were very offended that I inferred that their child was a sinner. Perhaps a quote from the Minnesota Crime Commission will help to prove the point to a doubter.

"Every baby starts life as a little savage. He is completely selfish and self-centered. He wants what he wants when he wants it—his bottle, his mother's attention, his playmate's toy, his uncle's watch. Deny him these wants, and he seethes with rage and aggressiveness, which would be murderous were he not so helpless. He is dirty. He has no morals, no knowledge, no skills. This means that all children, not just certain children, are born delinquent. If permitted to continue in the self-centered world of his infancy, given free reign to his impulsive actions to satisfy his wants, every child would grown up a criminal, a thief, a killer, a rapist."[29]

It is appropriate to acknowledge that you are quoting someone else, but I find that it is not always appropriate to use that person's name. Unsaved people say some good things, but to your audience, it wouldn't be wise to mention that it was Adolph Hitler who said it! You might introduce that quote by saying, "A powerful leader once said… ." If someone asks you later who it was, you could tell them privately and explain why you chose to use the quote. On the other hand, an unsaved person's quote may add "fuel to your fire" so to speak, and it would be wise to use their name. A member of Led Zepplin once said, "Rock music is sex." For us, that's pretty good evidence against it.

You should ask yourself some questions about the person you are quoting before you decide to use the material. Does his or her experience or training qualify them to speak on this subject? Is his testimony based on first hand knowledge? Is this authority prejudiced? How will the audience regard his testimony? Do they know him? Do they respect him?

Use your creative imagination to introduce the quote. It doesn't take much effort to say, "Spurgeon said; Paul wrote; or the Bible says." It does take some effort, but it would be more highly effective to introduce the same quotations in these ways, "Written boldly into the Bible is the phrase...; Paul keenly felt that ...; This is what Charles Dickens was trying to tell us when he observed ...; You can see the significance of those words embedded in verse ten ..." Use quotations sparingly. Your sermon should not sound like a term paper!

Narration

Have you ever noticed that we never gossip about ideas? We gossip about people. People are a part of everything we talk about. Narration within a sermon describes the individuals and the events involved in the Bible accounts. Every page of the Scripture contains something about a person. Sometimes they are very obvious because they are crying or laughing, cursing or praying, while at other times they are obscure. In every text there is someone writing it and someone who is reading it. In every doctrine you will always find a personality. For example, grace—there is someone needing it and someone giving it.

Think about the parables of Jesus for a minute. You will have to stretch your mind hard to think of one without some person right in the middle of the story. Jesus used this tool continually and so should we. It is through this method that our audience is able to identify personality with truth.

John Hercus uses narration well as he makes us live with David as he wrote Psalm 24:

"David sat up straight, stretched his arms and yawned. It had been a day of rehearsing, going over the whole processional routine with musicians, the singers, and the ballet. The score and the choreography were well advanced, and David was more than satisfied. The psalm was good—short, clear, well-suited to the occasion. Hm-m-m-m-m… that was a good choice phrase about 'ascend the hill of the Lord… stand in His holy place.' Very good. It would make a fine background for work with the cymbals and trumpets and chorus.

"And those four conditions of entry into the holy place—they were just right. Terse, compact, neat. Clean hands, pure heart, no accent on trashy values, and no cheating or being deceitful. Yes, indeed, that checks a man out as fully and completely as you could wish.

"Clean hands… like his own clean hands…

"Suddenly a memory flashed into his mind. A memory of washing, washing, washing, those 'clean' hands of his trying to scrub away a bloody thing that could not be undone. How did it happen? Oh yes…"[30]

"A picture is worth a thousand words" and narration paints that picture in our mind. Narration is communication with imagination—it brings freshness to a familiar passage. Take some time to think about how you would describe what the following people were thinking or feeling in these Bible accounts:

Goliath upon the arrival of David to fight with him.

The woman at the well as Jesus began to talk with her.
Abel as Cain was coming to kill him.
The whale who swallowed Jonah!
The Egyptians as they were drowning chasing the Israelites.
The people inside the walls of Jericho.
Those who watched Lazarus come out of the grave.
Those who experience the Great Tribulation.
The person who is in Hell today!

Still think you are not going to be able to fill thirty minutes? Believe me, if you will take this chapter and apply it carefully to your Scripture text, you will be asking your song-leader to cut down on the hymns and let you preach!

Once you get that skeleton (your outline) in place, there are numbers of ways to cover the bones. Do not forget about other Scriptures. We have not discussed it here, but go back and think about what you read in chapter two. You can not beat God's Word anywhere you use it in the message. Remember, God "may" bless restatement, definition, explanation, facts and statistics, quotations, or narration; but He promises to "always" bless His Word—so use it liberally!

We also have not talked about illustrations yet because an entire chapter is needed to discover the effectiveness of this tool in preaching.

CHAPTER SIX

Challenging Through Illustrations

Years ago during a revival I was invited to eat supper at the home of a medical doctor and his family. They lived in an underground house. It was quite a unique structure and I am sure quite costly. I remember sitting at the table that night feeling depressed. The house was dark, dreary, and cold. The fellowship was not much better—there was a strained atmosphere among the family members. (Years later I would learn that the doctor killed his wife with an overdose of pills and went to jail.) Up until that time, I always thought a house underground would be kind of unique and attractive, but after spending those couple of hours in that house, I changed my mind. A house just does not seem right without windows to let in light.

We have built the foundation of our sermon (the introduction) and have labored to construct the skeletal walls (the outline) and have covered them with some materials; but if our sermon is to have proper form and function, we must add some windows. Thomas Fuller said, "Reasons are the pillars of the fabric of a sermon; but similitudes are the windows which give the best lights." Spurgeon added, "To every preacher of righteousness as well as to Noah, wisdom gives this command, 'A window shalt thou make in the ark.' You may build up laborious definitions and explanations and yet leave your hearers in the dark as to your meaning; but a thoroughly suitable metaphor will wonderfully clear the sense. The world below me is a glass in which I may see the world above. The works of God are the shepherd's calendar and the ploughman's alphabet. While we thus commend illustrations for necessary uses, it must be remembered that they are not the strength of a sermon any more than a window is the strength of a house; and for this reason, they should not be too numerous. Too many openings for light may seriously detract from the stability of the building. Very beautiful sermons are generally very useless ones. To aim at elegance is to court failure. It is possible to have too much of a good thing: a glass house is not the most comfortable of abodes… and has the great fault of being sadly tempting to stone-throwers. Our house should be built up with the substantial masonry of doctrine, upon the deep foundation of inspiration; its pillars should be of solid scriptural argument, and every stone of truth should be carefully laid in its place; and then the windows should be arranged in due order."[31]

Henry Ward Beecher lectured in 1872: "I believe it was Locke who inveighed against illustrations as the enemies of truth, as leading men astray by latent or supposed analogies; and yet I apprehend that the strictest and most formal processes of logical reasoning have led just as many men astray as ever illustrations did. You can perplex people, and you can, with great facility, make ingenious issues with illustrations; but so you can with everything else. They are liable to misuse, but no more than any other instrument of persuasion. If a man knows truth and loves it, if he is earnest in the inculcation of it, and if he never allows himself to state for truth that which he does not thoroughly believe to be true, the processes which he employs, whether analogies, causal reasoning, or illustrations the most poetical, will participate in the honesty of the man; and there is little risk that any one part will be mistaken more than any other."[32]

Windows like everything else in our building must look good (form) and be effective (function). Jesus was the Master of using perfect illustrations to communicate truth. They not only captivated His audience, but they allowed His hearers to relate to the truth He was preaching.

The Nature Of An Illustration

Illustrations Are Pleasing To The Audience

Illustrations engage the listener into the message. Let us be honest—we live in an entertainment age where people have a very short attention span. The illustration draws people's attention toward the sermon and keeps them listening. We are not entertainers, but as stated earlier, if no one is listening, the best sermon is of no value. The illustration makes listening enjoyable.

Illustrations Help To Instruct
Learning is accomplished by going from the "known" to the "unknown." When a preacher states a doctrine or principle of Scripture that is unknown to his audience, and he says, "It's like... ," he is taking the hearer to something he "knows" so that he can understand that which is up until now "unknown." By likening something that is "unknown" (spiritual application) to something that is already "known" (an experience of life) learning is accomplished.

It is very important, therefore, that we use illustrations that people are familiar with. (Otherwise we are attempting to take people from the "unknown" to the "unknown.") As men we are very familiar with "men" things like sports, cars, hunting, etc. To us, "tight end," "right guard," "PT," "slice," "teed off," "strike," "turnover," "high sticking," and "taking it to the house" all make perfect sense. But many women in the audience are still in the "unknown." Often it is important to give some information about the illustration so that it will indeed allow light on the truth.

The Reason For Illustrations

They Assist In Communication
When we build a sermon, our goal should not be to make the sermon easy to preach. Our task is to make the sermon easy to understand. Our audience should not have to "work" at getting something out of the sermon. Our responsibility is to work hard in preparation so that the truth is easily seen, applied, and ultimately obeyed.

Here is an illustration of an illustration: An illustration is like an ornament on a Christmas tree. It is not there to take up space or just look pretty in itself. The ornament is there to draw the onlooker to the tree. Too many ornaments will clutter and hide the beauty of the tree and thus make it unappreciated, while not enough ornaments exposes too many bare spots leaving the onlooker with the idea that "it needs something."

Very few people will follow your train of thought through an entire message without the help of an illustration. Some in your audience will be listening doubtfully or suspiciously or even ignorantly, and when the illustration sheds that light on the truth, there is a sense of relief as they see the point. This is why our illustrations must always be relevant to the point we are making, otherwise we are merely entertaining and in essence wasting time.

Illustrations Can Be A Bridge In Difficult Situations
Sometimes the illustration is an "invisible" tactic. There may be something you need to preach on and yet not want to hit specifically because someone in the audience may think that you are just preaching to them. An example would be that there are a few people in the congregation who smoke. You would like to help them understand that this is a hindrance to their testimony (not to mention, bad for their health), but you do not want to preach an entire message on smoking since the majority of the congregation does not have this problem. Thus, in a message on "Separation" or "Consecration" you could use an illustration about "smoking" as an invisible tactic to be of help. For instance, you might tell how Spurgeon smoked cigars for years until one day as he was walking to lunch, he spotted a sandwich board in front of a tobacco shop with his picture on it. The caption read: "Smoke the cigars that Spurgeon smokes." He quit

smoking immediately, recognizing that the testimony of the Lord was at stake.

Illustrations Help People Remember Truth
Over the years I have preached thousands of sermons to young people. Almost invariably, some teenager will come up during the week and say, "I really like your stories." I must confess, that still bothers me a little bit, but remember, "a picture is worth a thousand words." (This includes word pictures.) If an illustration is timely and appropriate, the audience will go away remembering the illustration. But most of the time, if they are asked what the application of that illustration was, they will remember that as well. If they can remember the picture—they will remember the truth.

You can serve meat—but it tastes better salted! Illustrations, like salt, will not only make the sermon taste better, but will also help to preserve it longer.

Illustrations Help People To Think
Our volition (action) is dependent on our affection (will) which is dependent on the cognitive (mind). If any change is going to take place, it must start with the person thinking differently. Perry G. Downs makes this point clear: "Education that leads to spiritual growth must communicate the truths of Scripture clearly. If people are to act like Christians, they must think like Christians. If people are to think like Christians, they must first know what Scripture says and what it requires of them… . They must reject the old ways of thinking and be trained to think according to scriptural principles… . It is not enough that they have a "born-again" experience; they must now be taught to think and live according to the realities of the kingdom of God."[33]

Illustrations help stimulate thinking through the use of imagination. They help the audience to imagine living the truth that they are hearing about. If a message is being preached on the "Power of Prayer" and an illustration is given of someone who prayed for many years for his spouse to be saved and miraculously she came to Christ, the person listening to this illustration begins to "think" that this same thing could happen in his family as a result of prayer. The illustration helps him to "think" and "believe" that the truth is possible. If the illustration is negative, it helps the audience imagine what it would be like to disobey and not live the truth they are hearing.

A sixteen year old girl attended a revival meeting of mine in southern Ohio. When I met her on Sunday evening, I noticed that the whole right side of her body had been badly burned. I did not ask her about it, as she was a first-time visitor, but simply invited her to come back each night. On Tuesday night I preached a message on Hell and used several illustrations to help show the truth of the Bible that Hell is a literal place of fire and brimstone. I will never forget hearing what that young lady told the pastor at the front of the church that night as she came forward. She said, "Pastor, I have already been through a terrible fire here on earth. I don't want to die without Christ and spend eternity in a place of fire and burning." She was wonderfully saved. The sermon's illustrations helped her to "think" about her own illustrations of how terrible Hell would be and led her to embrace the truth.

Illustrations Help The Audience To Rest
Have you ever sat through a service and when it was over you looked at your watch and realized that the preacher had been

preaching for an hour and a half? You were surprised because it did not seem that long at all. Have you ever been listening for what seemed like an hour and a half and realized as you looked at your watch that only ten minutes had gone by?

There is an art in being able to preach as long as you need to without the audience becoming weary with listening. No one, no matter how skilled, can hold an audience spellbound by using a monotone in either voice or thought. You must create variety in both. Your principles and points will appeal to the mind while your illustrations will appeal to the heart.

The more emotions you can preach to—humor, sadness, anger, burden, etc., the longer you can preach. While you are addressing one emotion, the others are resting. As a result, the audience will listen to a long sermon and think it was short. Illustrations are often the best tool to use to reach these various emotions.

Illustrations Can Reach Everyone In The Audience

Everyone in the audience should get something out of your message. The youngest child who can understand the English language should go away with something from the sermon. One of the easiest ways to do this is with illustrations. Children are drawn to pictures—but remember what those pictures are worth! Beecher remarks, "I have around my pulpit, and sometimes crowding upon the platform, a good many of the boys and girls of the congregation. I notice that, during the general statements of the sermon and the exegetical parts of it, introducing the main discourse, the children are playing with each other. One will push a hymn-book or a hat toward the other, and they will set each other laughing. That which ought not to be done is, with children, very funny and amusing. By and by I have occasion to use an illustration, and I happen to turn round and look at the children, and not one of them is playing, but they are all looking up with interest depicted on their faces. I did not think of them in making it, perhaps, but I saw, when food fell out in that way, that even the children were fed too."[34]

Sources For Illustrations

Illustrations Are Everywhere
One of the most common questions that is asked by young preachers iss "Where do you get all of your illustrations?" I was having lunch with a fellow evangelist one day and was relaying to him a humorous incident that had happened during a service. I said, "I was right in the middle of an illustration when..." He interrupted me by blurting out, "What was the illustration?" (I never did tell him, but I did make him listen to my funny story.)

Earlier we stated that as a preacher you must learn to think homiletically, and you must always be thinking! This is not only true with respect to "seed thoughts" for sermons but for illustrative material as well. The sources for illustrations are endless: The Bible, personal experience, personal observation, children, literature, history, hymns, novels, art, the media, other religions, nature, sports, the military, science, travel, hobbies, object lessons, quotations, and poems, to name a few.

Beecher writes: "A man's study should be everywhere—in the house, in the street, in the fields, and in the busy haunts of men. You see a bevy of children in the window, and you can form them into a picture in your mind. You may see a nurse, and the way she is dressed. You try to describe it. You look again, and make yourself a master of the details. By and by it will come up to you again itself, and you will be able to make an accurate picture of it, having made your observation accurate. Little by little, this habit will grow, until by and by, in later life, you will find that you command respect by your illustrations just as much as by arguments and analogies."[35]

The Delivery Of Illustrations

Illustrations Must Be Accurate
If you will lie to tell a good story, your audience will assume that you will lie about anything—including the Gospel. Always give the facts as accurately as possible. I have often told a story about a murder/suicide that happened in front of the church where I was preaching. The story really was quite unbelievable, but I always told it as accurately as I could. I had given the story one Sunday morning in a message, and that evening a man approached me and said, "I didn't believe that story you told this morning but I went home and got on the Internet and typed in the city, state, a few of the names you mentioned and the date." He pulled up the story from the local newspaper on that date. He said, "Bro. Goetsch, I read the newspaper account and it was almost word for word as you told the story this morning!" Whenever I told that story after that, if I saw some skepticism in the eyes of those listening, I would pause, and say, "Go home and get on the Internet—and I would give them the name of the newspaper and the date. Immediately you could see a look of trust on their faces as I would finish the story.

Illustrations Should Be Clear
Remember this is the part of the message that is supposed to be "known." Know the crowd you are preaching to and

make sure you are illustrating on their level. First-graders in Junior Church are not going to understand the make-up of an atom! Keep in mind, you are not trying to help yourself preach, but rather attempting to help them understand.

Illustrations Should Be Down To Earth
Don't be afraid to illustrate truth in an undignified manner. While preaching in Christian School chapels, I would often sense that there were young people who had made professions of faith and looked and acted like Christians but were not truly born again. I would preach a message entitled *Are you a Fake?* about Judas Iscariot who looked and acted like a Christian but was lost. I would illustrate by talking about my "teeth." I would say, "Aren't you glad that you have teeth? If we didn't have teeth, we wouldn't be able to smile." And I would smile real big and get them to smile. "Without teeth we wouldn't be able to enjoy eating our food." I would take out an apple from my pocket and begin eating it. "Without teeth we wouldn't have anything to brush every morning." I would remove a toothbrush from my pocket and start brushing my teeth. By this time I had their attention as they would be giggling and making remarks. I would say, "I'm so glad that I have teeth—but you know what? Two of these teeth are fake! They're just plastic—they are artificial—they're not real!" I would then reach into my mouth and pull out my two artificial front teeth! (My real ones got knocked out playing football.) Believe me, I had their attention and more importantly, I had made my point! I'll admit it was a little humiliating, especially in the evening service when the parents of those kids would come up to me and stare at my mouth as they asked me, "Did you really take out your teeth

in chapel?" But it was worth getting down on the level of those kids in order to make a point.

Illustrations Must Be Quick Hitting
People get frustrated today when you waste their time. The audience should not be thinking faster than the preacher and making the application before you can give the illustration. If that is the case, you don't need the illustration! The illustration is the quick blow of the hammer that drives the point of the message home. Strike cleanly and quickly. Do not over-drive it or you will damage the wood!

Illustrations Must Always Be Appropriate
While preaching on God's omniscience, one preacher said, "God is even in the trash can." While what he said was accurate—it was not appropriate. Appropriateness may vary with the age and gender of the audience. An illustration about how someone got hooked into pornography and committed a horrible crime may be appropriate with a group of mature men, but would not be so among elementary school children in school chapel.

We must avoid anything that is off-color or has a double meaning connotation. Avoid sexual inferences as there is already plenty of that poisoning the minds of people in our society. We should never be gender or ethnically insensitive. Something may be funny to us, but greatly offensive to others. You should never be crude or make fun of someone in the audience. There is no place for rudeness in the pulpit today. We are to "speak the truth in love" and I think the Lord would be pleased if that sensitivity would also include our illustrations. If you are going to make fun of someone—use yourself.

Illustrations Should Be Told Dramatically

Get into it! The audience should feel like they are "there" in the story. Don't just re-tell the story—re-live it! Watch how people in normal conversation relate things that are exciting, funny, or important. Look at their facial expressions, listen to their voice inflections. They are getting their point across with more than words.

Do not entertain. Cut away anything that is surplus in the story and does not aid in shedding light on the truth you are preaching. A sculptor was asked how he carved a statue of a lion without a model. He said, "I simply carved away anything that did not look like a lion."

The Best Illustrations

Personal Illustrations

The best illustrations are those that you have experienced personally. They are easier told because you were there. You are aware of all of the pertinent facts. They are believable because of the information you are sharing that you would not have had access to if you had not been there as a witness.

Do not make yourself the hero in every story you tell. In real life we get tired of people who are constantly talking about themselves. People will listen to you a lot longer if they realize that you are human just like they are. Do not be afraid to be transparent and share your failures. People relate more to your failures than they do to your successes. Everyone has been a failure at something in life, but not everyone has enjoyed success. Modesty goes a long way toward confidence.

Be careful not to violate a confidence in an illustration. People will not share their concerns with you if they are afraid they will be featured in your next sermon. Someone else's story may benefit hundreds of people, but if it ruins his life because it was told, it is not worth it. Perhaps it can be told in the "third person." It is often wise to ask people's permission to use an illustration that involves them.

Conclusion

Illustrations and stories can be fun to tell, but be careful. Remember, they are just windows and too much of a good thing makes for a poor structure. The following is taken from Dr. Martyn Lloyd Jones' book *Preaching and Preachers* and serves well as a concluding "caution" to this chapter.

Stories and illustrations are only meant to illustrate truth, not to call attention to themselves. This whole business of illustrations and story-telling has been a particular curse during the past 100 years. I believe it is one of the factors that accounts for the decline in preaching because it helped to give the impression that preaching was an art, an end in itself. There have undoubtedly been many who really prepared a sermon simply in order to be able to use a great illustration that had occurred to them or which they had read somewhere. The illustration had become the first thing; you then find a text which is likely to cover this. In other words, the heart of the matter had become the illustration. But that is the wrong order. The illustration is meant to illustrate truth, not to show itself, not call attention to itself; it is a means of leading and helping people to see the truth that you are proclaiming more clearly. The rule therefore should always be that the truth must be preeminent and have great prominence, and illustrations must be used carefully to that end alone. Our business is not to entertain people. People like stories, they like illustrations.

"A preacher should go into the pulpit to enunciate and proclaim the truth itself. This is what should be prominent, and everything else is but to minister to this end. Illustrations are just servants.

"If truth is forgotten, then we are in the realm of fantasy, not to say comedy. We are to make sure that everything we may have by way of gifts is always subordinate to the truth. I suggest that the preacher always knows himself when he is taking delight in the story or imagination itself rather than in what it is meant to illustrate. The moment that point is reached you must stop; because you are not concerned just to influence people or to move them; our desire must be that the truth should influence and move them."[36]

Chapter Seven

Convicting Conclusions

An experienced pilot knows that landing an airplane demands special concentration, so an able preacher understands that conclusions require thoughtful preparation. Like the pilot, a skilled preacher should never have uncertainty about where his sermon will land. Like a lawyer, a minister asks for a verdict. The congregation should see the idea entire and complete, and listeners should know and feel what God's truth demands of them.[37]

The closer the preaching gets to the invitation, the harder the devil works. He is well aware that we are going to be soon asking for that verdict called a decision. He will distract the audience in any way possible. Therefore as preachers we must work especially hard at finishing our "house" well. If the introduction served as our "foundation," and the outline, the "walls," etc., then we could say that the conclusion must serve as the "roof" of the structure. A bad roof can do a lot of damage to a perfectly fine house. Likewise a poor unprepared conclusion will ruin all of the work that we have already done!

What Is A Good Conclusion?

The conclusion should never be called the "application." It is our desire that conviction start with the reading of Scripture (that is why a whole chapter was devoted to that subject), and with the question purposed in the proposition. A good sermon will make application continuously throughout.

Jay Adams states, "Good conclusions, like good sermons, work toward the goal of achieving the 'telos' (purpose) of the sermon. Often, if the introduction was right to the point, the conclusion can be made in terms of the introduction itself, thus wrapping up the entire sermon in one bow.... The purpose of the conclusion is not merely to bring the sermon to an end. It does that. But the principle function that it serves is to capsulize and capitalize on the sermon 'telos.' The listener goes away with the conclusion, which always calls for some change on his part, in mind. It must be powerful. Weak conclusions leave the impression, rightly or wrongly, that the whole message was weak."[38]

The Makeup Of A Good Conclusion

Conclusions Must Be Well Prepared
The conclusion is no less important than the introduction. Adams states, "What you say in the conclusion is what

people usually take away with them. This fact alone shows you how vital the conclusion and its form can be.[39]

I have heard of preachers who prepare the conclusion first so that they are sure that everything in the sermon funnels toward the ultimate purpose of the message. That may not be necessary, but when you do construct the "roof," make sure it covers well the purpose you presented from the start and culminates with conviction in the hearer to obey the truth.

The Conclusion Should Be Brief

It is very frustrating to be on an airplane that is unable to land. Circling the airport several times is unsettling to say the least. This is not the time when you want the audience to become weary with listening. They should not be anxious for you to finish or distracted because you were about to land but decided to pull back on the throttle and go up for a few more new thoughts.

In a moment you are going to be asking them to respond in the invitation. You need their full attention! Remember, the devil is working harder than ever now, so you have got no time to waste or spend on non-essentials.

The Conclusion Should Be Varied

Avoid stereotyped endings like the plague! There are other ways to end besides saying, "And in conclusion…" or "Let me close by saying…" or "Finally…" Or worst of all, "We're almost finished, so stay with me." When you say that—you are finished! Here are a few suggestions that will give variety to your conclusion:

    The quoting of a verse from a hymn.
    An impressive and relevant poem.
    An apt quotation.

A searching question. (Perhaps the same one used in your proposition.)
A solemn incident or illustration.
A summation of the main points.

The Conclusion Must Be Real
Forced or artificial emotion should always be avoided anywhere in the sermon, but especially here. God despises hypocrisy and deception of any kind. If the heart of the preacher is moved as it ought to be by the truth he has preached, any emotion in the voice or manners will be natural rather than phony. Avoid a "pulpit tone." You should not sound any different in the pulpit than you do in real life. Be yourself!

Emotions will vary with each preacher—but they must be controlled. The story is told of a preacher who wept profusely as he addressed a crowd of boys. One boy whispered to his companion, "What's he crying for?" The other replied, "If you were up there and had nothing to say—you'd cry too!"

The Conclusion Should Be Personal
This is not a time for generalities. You must be specific. The devil is the author of confusion—not God—so do not help Satan by muddying the waters. This is not the time to introduce new material. Get to the verdict! Nathan left no doubt in David's mind as to the purpose of the story of the ewe lamb! No one in your audience should be wondering at this point who you are talking to, "Thou art the man!"

We must faithfully, fearlessly, and yet courteously drive home the truth to the intelligence, emotions, and will of the hearers. There can be no doubt left as to the audience's responsibility in the mater. You must press for the same decision that God convicted you with when you first came to the Scripture that you have just preached. Dr. Martyn Lloyd Jones stated, "Preaching is not preaching unless people are brought to a decision."

The Conclusion Should Avoid a Fleshly Appeal
"It is the spirit that quickeneth, the flesh profiteth nothing, the words that I speak unto you, they are spirit and they are life." (John 6:63) Human gimmicks, manipulation, and high pressure are not of God and will not produce lasting results. It is God's Word that you have preached; it is God's Holy Spirit that has convicted the heart; so now let God bring about the decision as well. "I have planted, Apollos watered; but God gave the increase. So then neither is he that planteth any thing, neither he that watereth; but God that giveth the increase." (I Corinthians 3:6-7) Do not get caught in the numbers game or trapped into preaching pragmatically—be faithful to God and His Word—He will give it success. Remember, He promised. (Isaiah 55:10-11)

The Conclusion Should Conclude
It seems obvious, but not always practiced. Your "finishing point" should coincide with your "stopping point." Do not go on after you have finished. One man remarked when asked what he thought of a preacher's sermon, "I thought he missed several wonderful opportunities to quit!" The following may not be bad advice, "Stand up; Speak up; and Shut up!"

Do Not Give Satan An Advantage
As stated earlier, the devil will do everything in his power to redirect the heart of people at this point in the sermon. He

will counter your every move—so stay on the offense. Do not be ignorant of his devices. Block his punches before he can land them.

If your message has been negative in nature, for instance on the subject of some sin, it is wise to conclude with the positive. The Bible is profitable for "reproof" but also for "correction and instruction." If you have exposed a sin, then mentioning forgiveness now will give people hope of a solution to their problem and not simply leave them condemned. We want people to be convicted—but we want that conviction to lead to conversion or change. People are often already aware of their problem and are sometimes convinced there is no hope. We must supply that hope from God's Word.

If you feel like there are objections or hindrances to the message you have preached, it is wise to diffuse these in your conclusion. For example, you may know that the hindrance to several people being saved is their friends. It would be wise to conclude with something like, "The fear of man bringeth a snare, but whoso putteth his trust in the Lord shall be safe." (Proverbs 29:25) Or, "Your friends can laugh you out of Heaven, but they can not laugh you out of Hell!"

Chapter Eight
Compassionate Delivery

The delivery of the sermon is the most dynamic moment of the preaching experience. In that moment all sermon preparation is brought to fruition or frustration. If the sermon is delivered effectively, the preacher, in grateful joy, forgets the hours of toil in preparation. But if the sermon fails, all the labor and study will seem like a heavy and useless burden. The gospel is a proclaimed gospel. Thus, a sermon is never a sermon until it is delivered. A minister is never a preacher until the message is communicated to others.[40]

Robinson states, "The effectiveness of our sermons depends on two factors: what we say, and how we say it. Both are important. Apart from life-related, biblical content we have nothing worth communicating; but without skillful delivery, we will not get our content across to the congregation. In order of significance the ingredients making up a sermon are thought, arrangement, language, voice, and gesture. In priority of impressions, however, the order reverses. Gesture and voice emerge as the most obvious and determinative."[41]

Communication is a two-way street. You can not play catch by yourself! There must be someone throwing the ball and someone catching it. Unfortunately, as preachers, I am afraid we do a lot of throwing—but sometimes I wonder if anyone is catching. Have you ever watched a dad with his two-year old son in the park playing catch? The kid has a major league glove on his hand that is bigger than he is. Dad stands back about five feet and throws the ball and it hits him right in the face. The kid starts bawling, but Dad is determined he is going to learn to catch the ball. So, he moves closer and closer until he is only inches away. As the glove dangles from the boy's little hand, Dad throws it right into the pocket—the ball is caught! Dad yells and screams in delight as if his son had just won the World Series with that "basket" catch!

Too many times, we whip the truth at the audience hoping they are spiritually athletic enough to make the catch. We need to be more like that dad, who does everything in his power to make sure that the ball is caught. For this to happen, it is going to take more than a well constructed sermon. We have got to put our entire being into throwing a perfect pitch! If you are convinced of the centrality of preaching, you will learn everything you can to improve your delivery, so that every sermon will be a perfect strike!

The Preacher's Personality

The First Law Of Preaching

We are not actors! Be yourself! What we are preaching should be based on personal conviction and how we are preaching should be based on our true personality. Spurgeon wrote, "Scarcely one man in a dozen in the pulpit talks like a man. You may go all around, to church and chapel alike, and you will find that by far the majority of our preachers have a holy tone for Sundays. They have one voice for the parlor and the bedroom, and quite another tone for the pulpit; so that, if not double-tongued sinfully, they certainly are so literally. The moment some men shut the pulpit door, they leave their own personal manhood behind them, and become as official as the parish beadle."[42]

The Preacher's Emotions

Delivery does not start with the voice or body, but with the spiritual maturity of the preacher. The level of spirituality will be seen in the eyes, the face, the voice, the gestures, the posture, and in the attitude displayed toward the audience. If there is a conflict between emotion and statement—emotion will be the most powerful and the most evident. You cannot hide fear, anger, bitterness, joy, etc. "A merry heart maketh a cheerful countenance." (Proverbs 15:13)

A preacher will be most effective in delivery when speaking from a sense of divine purpose and conviction. Charles R. Brown in his Yale lectures described the pulpit work of George MacDonald of London: "He read for the Scripture lesson that morning the eleventh chapter of Hebrews. When the time came for the sermon, he said: 'You have all heard about these men of faith. I shall not try to tell you what faith is—there are theological professors who can do that much better than I could do it. I am here to help you to believe.' Then followed such a simple, heartfelt, and majestic manifestation of the man's own faith in those unseen realities which are eternal, as to beget faith in the minds and hearts of all his hearers. His heart was in his work, and his delivery was effective because it rested back upon genuine beauty of his own inner life."[43]

The preacher must work on controlling the emotion of fear which will disturb his poise and hinder the delivery. The size of the crowd, the attitude of the crowd, and the content of the sermon can all cause a fear in the heart of the preacher. Lack of poise is easily detected by the audience—a flushed face, unsteady hands or knees, rapid or shallow breathing, a dry mouth, strained pitch, etc.—are all signs of fear. Extreme fear can result in forgetfulness or absolute inability to speak. But do not look for fear to be totally removed—it is tension that makes for readiness and zest in delivery. Someone once asked the late Dr. B. Myron Cedarholm if he still got nervous before he preached? He said, "I'd be nervous if I wasn't nervous!" I was preaching with Dr. Paul Levin at the Bill Rice Ranch in Murfreesboro, Tennessee. We were sitting on the platform and he seemed unusually nervous that night prior to his message. During the special music, I leaned over and whispered, "I'll be praying for you tonight, Dr. Paul, as you preach." He whispered back, "Thanks. You know, they say, just trust God. I do trust God, but I don't trust the devil!" That is a healthy fear!

There are several ways to improve poise:
    Thorough preparation
    Concern for your audience

Reliance upon God
A good attitude toward the situation
Relax physically as much as possible, especially your throat.

The Preacher's Earnestness
Spurgeon remarked, "If I were asked—What in a Christian minister is the most essential quality of securing success in winning souls for Christ? I should reply, 'earnestness,' and if I were asked a second or third time, I should not vary the answer, for personal observation drives me to the conclusion that, as a rule, real success is proportionate to the preacher's earnestness. Both great men and little men succeed if they are thoroughly alive unto God, and fail if they are not so."[44]

He later stated, "Hear how Whitefield preached, and never dare to be lethargic again. Winter says of him that 'sometimes he exceedingly wept, and was frequently so overcome, that for a few seconds you would suspect he never would recover; and when he did, nature required some little time to compose herself. I hardly ever knew him to go through a sermon without weeping more or less. His voice was often interrupted by his affections; and I have heard him say in the pulpit, "You blame me for weeping; but how can I help it, when you will not weep for yourselves, although your own immortal souls are on the verge of destruction, and, for aught I know, you are hearing your last sermon, and may never more have an opportunity to have Christ offered you?"'"[45]

Earnestness is not something you learn in the college classroom, but rather in your study alone with God as the message of truth (and the world's lack of it) grips your heart. When Jesus saw the multitudes, He was moved with compassion. (Matthew 9:36) Jude 22 reminds us that it is compassion that makes the difference.

My wife's mother, Fay Brock, died of cancer at the early age of fifty-six. On her deathbed a few days before she went to Heaven, she said, "If my death will bring my husband to Christ, I'm ready to go." As I preached her funeral, I could see that my father-in-law was under conviction, but he was not quite ready to be saved. Two weeks later, I was preaching a revival in the city where he lived. He came to the meetings (he had only been to church a handful of times prior to that) and on the second night raised his hand for prayer. The next morning, I had the wonderful privilege of leading him to Christ in his home. I will never forget what he said immediately after praying the sinner's prayer. He looked at me and said, "John, I only have one regret." Taken back a little by this, I said, "A regret? What would it be?" He said, "That I didn't do this a long time ago. Fay always wanted me to be saved." What made the difference? My sermons? A church? I do not think so. Compassion on the dying face of one who loved him and cared about his soul!

The Tools Of The Trade

The Preacher's Voice
The most important and oft-used tool of a preacher is his voice. Taking good care of your voice is part of the obligation that you accept when you answer the call to preach. Good speaking voices are developed in time just like any muscle in the body. If a professional football player pulled a hamstring muscle in his leg, he would not go outside and run wind sprints. He would rest it and nurture it back to health and then be careful when running the next time to properly

stretch that muscle so as not to re-injure it. As a preacher, your voice is as valuable to you as that football player's legs. You can not "play" without your voice!

The Production Of Speech
If we are going to take care of our voice, we must have a basic understanding of how it operates.

Respiration: Respiration is the act of breathing. Steadiness of vocalization, projection, rate, pitch, and poise all depend in part on proper breathing. When speaking, you must breathe from the diaphragm or the abdominal region rather than pulling air from your lungs only. You must be able to take in a large amount of air quickly and expel it slowly. Proper posture will aid you in breathing properly for preaching.

Phonation: Phonation involves pitch, range, and inflection. Improper phonation will cause you to lose your voice. Your normal speaking relaxed voice is your normal pitch. You can vary your pitch, range, or inflection for emphasis, but only as an exception rather than the norm. When you change your pitch for expressiveness and interpretation, be careful not to go too far from your normal speaking voice.

Resonation: Resonation has to do with the tone of your voice. A nasal, harsh, or breathy sound will be distractive to the audience. Most resonation problems are functional and can be corrected with good speech habits. Practice reading or speaking aloud, record your voice on a tape recorder if necessary, listen for the distractive sounds, and correct them.

Articulation: Sounds are shaped into words by the tongue, lips, and teeth. A lazy mouth will produce a slurred speech that is difficult to understand. Clearness of speech is absolutely essential to communication. Often being heard has little to do with volume, but rather articulation. Failure to open your mouth, or lack of flexibility in your facial area will add up to failure in articulation. Put a large marshmallow or two in your mouth and try to enunciate words clearly to someone else. This will force you to open your mouth wider and attain the flexibility you need.

Rate: Rate will need to vary with the size of the audience, the acoustics of the building, and the nature of the sermon. Generally, the larger the crowd and the more difficult the acoustics, the slower the rate needs to be. Often the sermon material will dictate a slower or faster rate. A good rule of thumb is: Proper rate is varied and rapid enough to show vitality, and slow enough to assure distinct articulation. The "dramatic pause" is a good tool for emphasis. Pauses are the punctuation marks of speech. "By your silence," said Rudyard Kipling, "you shall speak." The pause gives the audience a chance to think, feel, and respond. Be aware that the pause will seem longer to you as the speaker, than it will to the audience. Do not be afraid to pause—silence fuels conviction!

Variety: We must avoid a "sameness" of speech or monotone. Our goal is a conversational delivery. Go to a restaurant or someplace where people are sitting and talking. Just listen to their normal conversation and think about how people naturally change their voices to express themselves to their audience. That same kind of variety should characterize your delivery.

Every preacher should give attention to his voice. Every preacher should take a speech class somewhere in his training. (I have often said that the most valuable class I took in high school was typing, and the most valuable class I took in college was speech, because I use them both every day of my life.) Our voice is the God-given instrument for communicating the Gospel. Why should those who use their voices for lesser means (actors, rock stars, news anchors) be more diligent in this area than the preacher of the Word of God?

The Preacher's Body

Preaching involves more than your voice. If a perfect preacher existed, no one would know it, because the perfect preacher is one whose delivery is unnoticed in communication. Remember, we are not trying to call attention to "us." We are trying to call people's attention to the message. However, the preacher cannot afford to preach two messages—one with his sermon and another with his body. The best speaker is one who speaks "with" his body and thus by using his total personality communicates the message.

Very much can be communicated without a spoken word. In fact someone who has bothered to count them insists that we can produce 700,000 distinct elementary signs with our arms, wrists, hands, and fingers.[46] In Proverbs 6:13, God speaks of a wicked man who, "… winketh with his eyes, he speaketh with his feet, he teacheth with his fingers;" When actor George Arliss first read the play "Disraeli," he advised the author to take out two pages. "I can say that with a look," he said. "What look?" asked the author. Arliss demonstrated, and the pages came out.[47]

Spurgeon stated, "We cannot express so much by action as by language, but one may express a few things with even greater force. Indignantly opening a door and pointing to it is quite as emphatic as the words, 'Leave the room!' To refuse the hand when another offers his own is a very marked declaration of ill-will, and will probably create a more enduring bitterness than the severest words. A request to remain silent upon a certain subject could be well conveyed by laying the finger across the lips. A shake of the head indicates disapprobation in a very marked manner. The lifted eyebrows express surprise in a forcible style; and every part of the face has its own eloquence of pleasure or grief. What volumes can be condensed into a shrug of the shoulders, and what mournful mischief that same shrug has wrought! Since, then, gesture and posture can speak powerfully, we must take care to let them speak correctly."[48]

God designed the body to move. If a congregation wants to look at a statue, they can go to a museum. Even there, however, the most impressive statues are those that appear alive. In most realms the professional uses his whole body. The conductor of a symphony, the concert pianist, the baseball pitcher, the umpire, the actor, the golfer all put their bodies into what they do. An accomplished speaker likewise lets his body speak for him.[49]

Here are some particular areas of the preacher's body that should be given special attention:

Appearance: Someone has suggested that 70 percent of a person's impression of you is determined in the first thirty seconds he see you! First impressions are important. You are preaching long before you stand in the pulpit and speak. There are three basic rules: conservative, neat, and clean. Don't try to be trendy—we want people to focus on the sermon, not your multi-colored Tweetie Bird tie! John

Chapter Eight - Compassionate Delivery

T. Molloy, wardrobe consultant to many of America's top corporations, has been asked if any traits are common to all successful executives. He emphasizes two: their hair is combed and their shoes are shined. And they expect the same of other men, particularly subordinates. Molloy's studies indicate that disheveled hair, even if short, triggers strong negative reactions in other men.[50] A minister does not prove he is an expository preacher by looking as though he dressed staring into a Greek lexicon instead of the mirror!

Posture: Your posture begins with how you sit on the platform. Exhibit physical alertness on the platform. Show an interest in everything that is taking place in the service. Once in the pulpit, your weight should be distributed evenly on your feet. Avoid swaying back and forth or rocking on your toes. Do not slouch or lean against the pulpit and work conscientiously at keeping your hands out of your pockets!

Eye Contact: The eye is the window into the soul. You must at least give the impression that you are looking into the eyes of your listeners. (If their eyes scare you—look at the bridge of their nose—you will be close enough!) Do not look at one person too long—keep your eyes moving across the congregation. Avoid looking at the floor, the ceiling, or out the window, etc. Good eye contact gives the listener assurance that you desire to communicate. Again, Spurgeon makes the point clear, "The face, and especially the eyes, will play a very important part in all appropriate action. It is very unfortunate when ministers cannot look at their people. It is singular to hear them pleading with persons whom they do not see.... It seems to me that you must fix your eyes upon the people when you come to exhortation. There are parts of a sermon in which the sublimity of the doctrine may call for the uplifted gaze, and there are other portions which may allow the eyes to wander as you will; but when pleading time has come, it will be inappropriate to look anywhere but to the persons addressed."[51]

Gestures: Gestures involve the whole body—the arms and hands, but also the head, the shoulders and the eyes. All gestures should be motivated from within and be natural, never forced or artificial. They should be coordinated with the rest of the body and the flow of the message. Make your gestures appropriate to the occasion, the size of the crowd, and the nature of the sermon. Do not get into a rut—vary your gestures. Watch yourself on video to see where your "comfort zone ruts" are.

There are four conventional gestures: The index finger is used for location and mild emphasis. A clenched fist is used for dramatic or strong emphasis. The "palms up" gesture is used to suggest affirmative or pleading emotion. The "palms down" gesture signals disapproval, rejection, and contempt.

There are three "planes" of gestures: The "upper" plane—from the shoulder up—and is expressive of the most powerful and reverent thoughts. The "middle" plane—from the shoulders to the waist—is most often used and where almost all emotions can be expressed adequately. The "lower" plane—from the waist down—expresses negative thoughts.

General Body Movement: Too much body movement is distractive. Changes in position should be natural, except when doing something unusual for emphasis. A change in position can be especially effective when making a transition in thought, such as when you move from one point to another in the sermon. Mannerisms should be avoided such as tugging at your clothing, hands in your pockets, hands behind you, leaning on the pulpit, etc. These can all be used for some kind of emphasis but should not be the norm. Video taping yourself will reveal the gestures you use or don't use. Or, if you really want to know—ask your wife—but be prepared!

Conclusion

Delivery is something that is very difficult to teach in preaching because it must come from within, being motivated by the message. If there is no voice inflection, body movement, raised volume from time to time, etc., the message probably does not mean much to you. But when there is a "fire" burning in your bones and it has to get out—it will be evident in your delivery!

Do not try to copy someone else, but watch others as they preach. What is effective in their delivery that you would feel comfortable doing? Do not just listen to other preachers—watch them! Be yourself, but be willing to change yourself to be more effective in communicating God's message. Delivery is what draws the audience's attention into the truth we are preaching. Charles Finney was once asked by a New York newspaper if they could print his sermons? He replied, "Sure, you can print the sermon—but you can't print the fire! May God give us today some of that unprintable fire!

CHAPTER NINE

Conducting the Invitation

If you have read everything up to this point, I hope it is obvious that I believe in letting God do His work through His message rather than through man's methods! Nothing changes at this point. We are responsible to prepare and deliver the Word; the Holy Spirit has the responsibility to draw men to the Saviour. I have always believed that the preacher must be extremely sensitive to the leading of the Holy Spirit in the giving of the invitation. We cannot dictate to God how He should work in people's hearts or in what manner they should make a decision. However, too much is at stake, and too much time has already been invested in the preaching process to have the attitude of "whatever" at the invitation.

There are many different opinions, ideas, thoughts, and methods with respect to this part of the preaching service. There are some that believe giving an invitation is unscriptural. Others feel comfortable with a very low-key approach, while still others would consider this the most important part of the service.

Is An Invitation Scriptural?

The Bible Word: "Come"

Often during an invitation, the word "come" is used. "Come forward." "Come to the altar." "Come and receive Christ." It is amazing how often we find that word in the Bible as God encourages people to respond to His message.

Genesis 7:1	"And the Lord said unto Noah, Come thou and all thy house into the ark…"
Isaiah 1:18	"Come now, and let us reason together, saith the Lord: though your sins be as scarlet, they shall be as white as snow; though they be red like crimson, they shall be as wool."
Matthew 11:28	"Come unto me, all ye that labour and are heavy laden, and I will give you rest."
Revelation 22:17	"And the Spirit and the Bride say, Come. And let him that heareth say, Come. And let him that is athirst come. And whosoever will, let him take the water of life freely."

Chapter Nine - Conducting the Invitation

Jesus lamented the fact that some would not come to Him. "O Jerusalem, Jerusalem... how often would I have gathered thy children together, even as a hen gathereth her chickens under her wings, and ye would not." (Matthew 23:37) And again in John 5:40, "And ye will not come to me, that ye might have life."

Nowhere in the Gospels does Jesus encourage an inward or private decision. In fact, in Matthew 10:32-33, He says quite the opposite, "Whosoever therefore shall confess me before men, him will I confess also before my Father which is in heaven. But whosoever shall deny me before men, him will I also deny before my Father which is in heaven."

In the first century, preachers encouraged a public decision. In the Book of Acts, the converts were always admonished to be baptized immediately, which as we know, is the outward testimony of what has taken place in the heart. On the day of Pentecost, Peter exhorted: "... Repent, and be baptized every one of you in the name of Jesus Christ...," and "... they that gladly received his word were baptized: and the same day there were added unto them about three thousand souls." (Acts 2:38, 41) In Acts 8:38, we find Philip as he "... commanded the chariot to stand still: and they went down both of them into the water, both Philip and the eunuch; and he baptized him." And later, the Philippian jailor in chapter sixteen of Acts "... took them the same hour of the night, and washed their stripes; and was baptized, he and all his, straightway." (verse 33)

From these Scriptures, we can confidently say that it would not be unbiblical to give an invitation publicly for people to come to Christ. There are many Old Testament Scriptures that can also be cited where the people upon hearing the Word of God made a public declaration of their intention to obey. Joshua stood before his people publicly and declared, "...As for me and my house, we will serve the Lord." (Joshua 24:15) After hearing the Word of God read in II Chronicles 34, King Josiah "... stood in his place, and made a covenant before the Lord, to walk after the Lord, and to keep his commandments, and his testimonies, and his statues, with all his heart, and with all his soul, to perform the words of the covenant which are written in this book." (verse 31) Verse 32 then says, "And he caused all that were present in Jerusalem and Benjamin to stand to it... ."

Walking An Aisle Does Not Make or Break the Decision
A decision is no more "real" because a person walks an aisle, nor does not walking the aisle make a decision "unreal." Walking the aisle publicly may, however, be important to break the person's will.

The late Evangelist Fred Brown told me this story. A young lady attended his meetings several nights in a row. He noticed that the first night she attended, she raised her hand indicating that she was not saved and wanted prayer. However, when the invitation was given, she did not respond. Dr. Brown saw her after the service and asked her if she would like to be saved. She said, "Yes, but I'm not walking that aisle!" Dr. Brown then said, "Well, then, you cannot be saved." She returned the next night and again raised her hand but refused to come forward. Again, after the service, when Dr. Brown asked her if she would like to be saved, she said, "Yes, but I'm not going to walk down that aisle!" Again, Dr. Brown told her, "Then you cannot be saved."

This same thing happened for several nights in a row until finally after the last service of the week, the young lady

Chapter Nine - Conducting the Invitation | 103

simply sat down in the pew at the close of the invitation and began to weep. Dr. Brown approached her and as he did, she looked up at him through her tears and said, "Dr. Brown, I'm ready now to walk the aisle and be saved." He said, "Good, now you don't have to," and he led her to Christ in her seat!

One of the saddest experiences I have ever had was one night in Phoenix, Arizona. When I asked for heads to be bowed at the close of the message, I asked if there were those there who were not sure of eternal life and would like me to pray for them. If so, I asked them to slip up their hand. About half way back on the left hand side, sitting on the seat closest to the aisle, a ten-year old girl raised her hand. I can still see that sweet little girl with her blonde hair and her blue eyes looking up at me as she raised her hand. She no more than got her hand in the air, when her mother noticed it and reached over and pulled her hand down. With heads still bowed, I asked the pianist to begin playing an invitation song, and I invited those who needed to be saved to come forward and speak to the pastor. The little girl made a step toward the aisle to come, but got no further, as her mother grabbed her by the shoulder, pushed her down in the seat, and scolded her for her attempt to come forward.

As the invitation continued, I did my best to explain that a person could get saved right there in his seat by confessing that he were a sinner and asking Jesus Christ by faith to save him. I honestly believe that I will see that little girl in Heaven one day. She never walked an aisle, but salvation takes place in the heart by faith. I truly hope that her mother also came to her senses, and to the Saviour, lest it be better that a millstone were hanged about her neck and she be cast into the depth of the sea and be drowned (Matthew 18:6).

When people do come forward, we do have the opportunity to give further explanation and help to them as they make their decision. Often people know "what" they need to do, but are not always sure "how" and coming forward affords them the help they need.

Guidelines For The Invitation

The Invitation Should Be In Harmony With The Message
We started with a convicting question way back in the introduction with our proposition. This is no time to "change horses!" Since the moment you read Scripture, everything has been pointed at this target. The invitation should thus flow naturally from the message. You should not be wondering at this point what you are going to ask the audience to respond to. In fact, the audience will not be wondering either—they will have known long before now what God's Word is instructing them to do.

Certainly the Holy Spirit can speak to the hearts of people about areas not mentioned in the sermon—it happens quite often—but "you" are not the Holy Spirit. "He who aims at nothing, hits it every time." You have carefully in preparation loaded your ammunition, spent the entire sermon aiming your delivery at the target—do not be distracted now—squeeze the trigger with the bulls-eye in the sight!

The Invitation Should Be Clear
Be simple, speak slowly, and articulate carefully your instructions to people in the invitation. Remember, Satan will confuse—he "invented" confusion. I was standing in the lobby of a church one night after preaching and a

man approached me and said, "I would have come forward tonight to be saved, but I thought you wanted me to join the church first." I could not believe it! I never even mentioned joining a church that night. I went back and listened to the tape—not one mention of joining a church in the entire service! Who put that thought in that man's mind? Satan did not want him to be saved and was throwing every obstacle he could in his path.

You know exactly what you want people to do. You know the procedure of coming forward, talking to a counselor, seeing what God's Word has to say, praying and making a decision. But the average person today in our post-Christian culture has no idea what he needs to do to quench the thirst in his soul for God. Help him by being clear!

The Invitation Should Be Simple
Hand in hand with clarity is simplicity. If you are asking people to raise their hands indicating needs in their lives, it is best to ask them to respond to one thing at a time. This helps them to focus in on what the Holy Spirit wants them to do and it helps you to pray specifically for their needs.

This is not the time to show off your theological vocabulary! "Come," "trust," "believe," "obey," "seek," "turn," and "receive" are all words a child understands. Use them.

Do Not Try To Create A "Mood" For The Invitation
If you are still fishing around for some manipulative method to get someone down the aisle at this point, you are in big trouble. Have some music—sure; pray sincerely and compassionately—absolutely; lovingly persuade—without question: but humanly, this is the time to step back out of the way and let the Holy Spirit use His Word that has been

faithfully preached. "No man can come to me, except the Father which hath sent me draw him..." (John 6:44) "So then faith cometh by hearing, and hearing by the Word of God." (Romans 10:17)

Give Ample Time For The Invitation
In our fast-paced world, we are always in a hurry. We live by a schedule and are bound to time constraints. But don't abort the baby! Have you ever been around a young couple that is expecting their first child? They tell everyone that they are expecting! You ask them, "When?" and they say, "In eight and a half months!" You go to their house and the baby's room has already been prepared—the crib is in place, diapers are neatly stacked on the shelf along with a football helmet. A suitcase sits by the door neatly packed with Mom's clothes for the hasty trip to the hospital. If you have four or five kids of your own, you are thinking—these people better get a grip!

I know you are anxious for results—if you weren't—you would not be fit for the ministry. "Knowing therefore the terror of the Lord, we persuade men..." (II Corinthians 5: 11) "Brethren, my heart's desire and prayer to God for Israel is, that they might be saved." (Romans 10:1) Physical birth takes nine months and any attempt to take that child before full-term is greatly discouraged. Abortion is sin and when children must be born prematurely, their growth rate is greatly hindered. Like good parents, we must be patient to produce healthy and strong decisions.

Never rush the Holy Spirit's work for the sake of convenience or necessity. Remove something else from the service or the sermon to allow enough time for the invitation to be conducted properly and for people to be dealt with carefully. Never hurry a decision just to get a card so that it can be announced to the congregation.

In conclusion, let me say that the invitation is a sensitive time in the lives of the people who have heard God's Word. We must be careful not to interfere with the work of the Holy Spirit and at the same time not to be negligent in giving people an opportunity to respond. Time should be spent in prayer, weighing carefully how the invitation for each sermon should be worded and conducted. Souls and lives are in the balance in these moments. It is our utmost responsibility to do all that we can to allow the Holy Spirit to do His work in hearts.

The words of Spurgeon again seem appropriate here, "Consider the great evil which will certainly come upon us and upon our hearers if we be negligent in our work. 'They shall perish'—is not that a dreadful sentence? It is to me quite as awful as that which follows it—'but their blood will I require at the watchman's hand.' How shall we describe the doom of an unfaithful minister? And every unearnest minister is unfaithful. I would infinitely prefer to be consigned to Tophet as a murderer of men's bodies than as a destroyer of men's souls; neither do I know of any condition in which a man can perish so fatally, so infinitely, as in that of the man who preaches a gospel he does not believe, and assumes the office of pastor over a people whose good he does not intensely desire. Let us pray to be found faithful always, and ever. God grant that the Holy Spirit may make and keep us so."[52]

Chapter Ten
Character of Preachers

"Your talk talks; and your walk talks; but your walk talks louder than your talk talks." "Your actions are so loud, I can't hear what you are saying."

Preachers are sinners saved by God's grace—we are far from perfect. But the people who listen to us preach will hold us to a higher standard. Preaching is a "public" ministry and our audience will watch how we live outside the pulpit. It is vital that we not only attempt to "do" something for God, but that we "are" something with God. Being a good preacher starts with being a good Christian. So, regardless of whether or not we have mastered homiletics, every one of us must be growing in our walk with God or the most masterfully crafted sermon will be a miserable failure. It takes a lifetime to build a good name, and about five minutes to ruin it!

Character does matter—in fact, it always has. In February of 1895, Dr. David H. Greer spoke the following words to the preachers at Yale University, "Instead, therefore, of making much of individuals today, we put our trust in corporations, in institutions, in organizations, in machines; the individual man becoming less and less important, shrinking into smaller and smaller proportions, gradually going down into the depths of obscurity and darkness, dropping out of sight and mind. The corporation is everything, the individual nothing; socially great and strong, personally weak and unimportant. Never let your work come between you and God. You will be tempted to do so at times; but do not yield to that temptation. Let nothing come between you and God; for it is as men of God that you go. Men of God! Think how much that means, or how much it ought to mean. Thus, and only thus, laying hold on God, will you become in a measure the incarnation of God, His quickening power and life flowing into your souls. Thus, and only thus, will you most effectively do what He, who was on earth both Son of Man and God, has sent you forth to do."[53]

Dr. James Stalker lectured at Yale in 1891 saying, "There are many motives which may go to constitute a powerful ministry and enable us to rejoice in our vocation. But far more important than them all is a strong personal attachment to the Saviour. This is the motive of the ministry which goes deepest and wears longest." When Jesus' "love is burning in their very bones… the life of Christ in them cannot help manifesting itself after its kind." He then quoted the following hymn, believed to be written by St. Patrick,

> Christ with me, Christ before me,
> Christ behind me, Christ within me,
> Christ beneath me, Christ above me,
> Christ at my right, Christ at my left,
> Christ in the fort,
> Christ in the chariot seat,
> Christ in the heart of every man who thinks of me,
> Christ in the mouth of every man who speaks to me,
> Christ in every eye that sees me,
> Christ in every ear that hears me.[54]

The prince of preachers, Spurgeon, was not silent on this matter. Although he excelled in eloquence, oratory, and preaching abilities, he recognized all too well that a holy man must preach a holy God:

"We desire to rise to the highest style of ministry, and if so, even if we obtain the mental and oratorical qualifications, we shall fail, unless we also possess high moral qualities. There are evils which we must shake off, as Paul shook the viper from his hand, and there are virtues which we must gain at any cost. Self-indulgence has slain its thousands; let us tremble lest we perish by the hands of Delilah. Let us have every passion and habit under due restraint: if we are not masters of ourselves we are not fit to be leaders in the church. We must put away all notion of self-importance. God will not bless the man who thinks himself great. To glory even in the work of God the Holy Spirit in yourself is to tread dangerously near to self-adulation. 'Let another man praise thee, and not thine own lips.'

"Count nothing little which even in a small degree hinders your usefulness; cast out from the temple of your soul the seats of them that sell doves as well as the traffickers in sheep and oxen.... . Resolve, dear brethren, that you can be poor, that you can be despised, that you can lose life itself, but that you cannot do a crooked thing... .

"In a word, we must labour for holiness of character. What is holiness? Is is not wholeness of character? A balanced condition in which there is neither lack nor redundance? You must have holiness; and, dear brethren, if you should fail in mental qualifications (as I hope you will not), and if you should have a slender measure of the oratorical faculty (as I trust you will not), yet, depend upon it, a holy life is, in itself, a wonderful power, and will make up for many deficiencies; it is, in fact, the best sermon the best man can deliver. Let us resolve that all the purity which can be had we will have, that all the sanctity which can be reached we will obtain, and that all the likeness to Christ that is possible in this world of sin shall certainly be in us through the work of the Spirit of God."[55]

If holiness of life and character was the prime essential for preachers over one hundred years ago, could it be any less important for us in the 21st century? In fact, the Apostle Paul addresses this matter in his first letter to Timothy in the first century. Seven times Paul uses the word "thyself" in his letter, and each time it has significance to the preacher and his character.

A Preacher's Self-Discipline

Behave Thyself

"But if I tarry long, that thou mayest know how thou oughtest to behave thyself in the house of God, which is the church of the living God, the pillar and ground of the truth." (I Timothy 3:15) The preacher ought to be the best example of his preaching. "He who would be a good "conductor" must first himself be characterized by good "conduct." "In all things shewing thyself a pattern of good works." (Titus 2:7)

Exercise Thyself
"But refuse profane and old wives' fables, and exercise thyself rather unto godliness." (I Timothy 4:7) The Greek word for "exercise" is the word "gumnazo" from which we get our word gymnasium and gymnastics. The preacher must maintain a consistent spiritual exercise in four areas:
1. He must have an exercised conscience: "And herein do I exercise myself, to have always a conscience void of offense toward God, and toward men." (Acts 24:16)
2. He must have an exercised mind: "But strong meat belongeth to them that are of full age, even those who by reason of use have their senses exercised to discern both good and evil." (Hebrews 5:14)
3. He must have an exercised spiritual life: "... exercise thyself rather unto godliness." (I Timothy 4:7)
4. He must have an exercised physical body: "For bodily exercise profiteth little..." (for a little time). (Timothy 4:8) Preaching is physical work and requires physical fitness.

Give Thyself
"Meditate upon these things; give thyself wholly to them, that thy profiting may appear to all." (I Timothy 4:15) What costs nothing, gives nothing, does nothing, and is worth nothing! "And I will very gladly spend and be spent for you; though the more abundantly I love you, the less I be loved." (II Corinthians 12:15) "Even as the Son of man

came not to be ministered unto, but to minister and to give his life a ransom for many." (Matthew 20:28)

Take Heed Unto Thyself
"Take heed unto thyself, and unto the doctrine, continue in them: for in doing this thou shalt both save thyself, and them that hear thee." (I Timothy 4:16) In this verse, Paul tells Timothy to take heed to sound doctrine, but before he places emphasis on right doctrine, he tells him to take heed to right living. Good doctrine coming from wrong lives produces nothing.

Suppose you were extremely hungry and you had the money to eat at any restaurant in the world. And suppose you just so happened to be in a city where the number one steakhouse in the world was located. This restaurant has been written about in all of the travel and food magazines, the chef is world renowned. So, you get in your car and you make your way to this world-famous establishment. It takes you awhile to find it, and by the time you park your car, you are absolutely starved! As you walk up to the front door, you notice that there is a small hamburger joint right next door to the steakhouse. You think, you know, it is going to be another hour or so before I get to eat. By the time I get a table, order my meal, and it is served—I will be dead of starvation! Maybe I should slip into the hamburger joint and get a quick burger to tide me over.

As you contemplate this decision, you decide to walk around the block and think about it. As you make your way around behind these two buildings you notice that there is a window in the back of the steakhouse looking into the kitchen where the food is being prepared. There he is—that world renowned chef! As you watch him, you notice that his hands are extremely dirty (it looks like he changed the oil on his pick-up just before coming in to work), his fingernails are extremely long and curled over, his greasy hair is dangling down into the lettuce that he is chopping up for a salad, and his apron is splattered with blood and food particles.

You move on, only to notice that in the back of the hamburger joint, there is a similar window, looking into the grill area. There you notice a young kid, probably sixteen or so, flipping hamburgers. It's probably his first job, but as you observe him, you notice that his hands are sparkling clean, his short hair is tucked neatly under a cap, and his apron is dazzling white!

Now, let me ask you, "Where are you going to eat?" I believe I will have a hamburger! The finest steak served by a filthy cook has no appeal. And neither does the pure doctrine of God coming from preachers whose character is not pure. A preacher's worst enemy is himself. D.L. Moody remarked, "My worst enemy is the man who walks underneath my hat." When Abraham Lincoln was asked if he feared any of his opponents for the presidency of the United States, he replied, "Yes, one. I fear a man named Lincoln. If I am defeated, I will be defeated by him." George Mueller, the great example of faith, prayed, "Lord, deliver me from becoming a dirty old man."

"Watch and pray, that ye enter not into temptation...." (Matthew 26:41) The disciples did not watch, and they didn't pray, but instead fell asleep and thus fell to temptation. The preacher should be careful to be on "watch" in at least four areas:
1. Watch your words: lest like Moses you speak "...unadvisably with his lips." (Psalms 106:33)

2. Watch your friends: because "evil communications corrupt good manners." (I Corinthians 15:33)
3. Watch your habits: because we must "abstain from all appearance of evil." (I Thessalonians 5:22)
4. Watch our opportunities: because "as we have therefore opportunity, let us do good unto all men, especially unto them who are of the household of faith." (Galatians 6:10)

Save Thyself
"Take heed unto thyself, and unto the doctrine; continue in them: for in doing this thou shalt both save thyself, and them that hear thee." (I Timothy 4:16) This is not speaking of salvation, but rather of saving ourselves from loss at the Judgment Seat of Christ. "Every man's work shall be made manifest: for the day shall declare it, because it shall be revealed by fire; and the fire shall try every man's work of what sort it is. If any man's work abide which he hath built thereupon, he shall receive a reward. If any man's work shall be burned, he shall suffer loss: but he himself shall be saved; yet so as by fire." (I Corinthians 3:13-15) "Look to yourselves, that we lose not those things which we have wrought, but that we receive a full reward." (II John 8)

Keep Thyself
"Lay hands suddenly on no man, neither be partaker of other man's sin: keep thyself pure." (I Timothy 5:22) The preacher must be careful to keep himself in at least four areas:
1. Keep from immorality: "But I keep under my body, and bring it into subjection: lest that by any means, when I have preached to others, I myself should be

a castaway." (I Corinthians 9:27) Both Samson and Solomon are men that did not do well in this area.
2. Keep from idols: "Little children, keep yourselves from idols." (I John 5:21) Anything that displaces God from His rightful place is an idol.
3. Keep from growing cold: "Keep yourselves in the love of God…" (Jude 21) The preacher's heart must always be warm "speaking the truth in love."
4. Keep from worldliness: "… and to keep himself unspotted from the world." (James 1:27) Though we are "in" the world, we must not allow the world to be "in" us.

Withdraw Thyself
"… from such withdraw thyself." (I Timothy 6:5) The preacher must avoid anything and anyone who would hinder him from serving God. "Wherefore seeing we also are compassed about with so great a cloud of witnesses, let us lay aside every weight, and the sin that doth so easily beset us, and let us run with patience the race that is set before us." (Hebrews 12:1)

The Preacher's Self-Watch

In his second letter to Timothy, Paul warns the young preacher, to "watch" every area of his life. "But watch thou in all things…" (II Timothy 4:5) Because the preacher lives in a "glass house" and everyone is able to look through that glass and watch his life, he is wise to look often in the glass of his mirror and observe himself. "But let a man examine himself.… For if we would judge ourselves, we should not be judged." (I Corinthians 11:28, 31) This will hold true at the judgment before God, but will serve us well here on earth before our fellow man as well.

Watch Your Manners
The preacher must always have a humble spirit. Paul reminds us that Christ "… made himself of no reputation…" (Philippians 2:7) and Jesus Himself stated in Luke 22:27 "… but I am among you as he that serveth." The following poem is entitled "The Faithful Preacher" and most fittingly bears as its source, "Author Unknown."

"The Faithful Preacher"
He held the lantern, stooping low,
So low that none could miss the way;
And yet so high to bring in sight,
The picture fair, the world's great light:
The gazing up, the lamp between,
The hand that held it scarce was seen.

He held the pitcher, stooping low,
To lips of little ones below,
He raised it to the weary saint,
And bade him drink, when sick and faint.
They drank, the pitcher thus between,
The hand that raised it scarce was seen.

He blew the trumpet soft and clear,
To call the waiting soldier near;
And then with louder note and bold,
To raze the walls of Satan's hold.
The trumpet coming thus between,
The hand that raised it scarce was seen.

Chapter Ten - Character of Preachers

But when the Captain says, Well Done,
Thou good and faithful servant come.
Lay down the pitcher and the lamp,
Lay down the trumpet, leave the camp.
The weary hands will then be seen,
In his pierced hands, with naught between.
                              -Author Unknown

The preacher must also be courteous. The word "tact" means "touch" as in contact. Everyone who comes in contact with the man of God should be touched, but not offended by rudeness or impoliteness. "Giving no offense in anything… that the ministry be not blamed." (II Corinthians 6:3) Talent knows "what" to say—tact knows "how" to say it. Talent makes a man "respectable"—tact makes him "respected."

Watch Your Language

If our voice is our greatest tool, then we must be careful what we craft with it. "A word fitly spoken is like apples of gold in pictures of silver." (Proverbs 25:11) "The preacher sought to find out acceptable words… even words of truth." (Ecclesiastes 12:10) We must always remember that God is our first audience—He hears every word we say. Thus, "Let the words of my mouth, and the meditation of my heart, be acceptable in thy sight, O Lord, my strength, and my redeemer." (Psalm 19:14)

Simplicity is an area we have mentioned several times, but it is important in our words. Understanding is essential to obedience. Illumination is essential to edification. Paul wrote, "So likewise ye, except ye utter by the tongue words easy to be understood, how shall it be known what is spoken?" (I Corinthians 14:9)

"Big, high-sounding words are often graves in which men bury their little ideas."

Of one preacher it was said, "He went down deeper, stayed down longer, and came up drier than any man I ever heard!" Which would you rather hear?

Twinkle, twinkle, little star,
How I wonder what you are:
Up above the world so high,
Like a diamond in the sky.

Or

Scintillate, scintillate, globule vivific,
Fain would I fathom thy nature specific,
Loftily poised in the ether capacious,
Strongly resembling a gem carbonaceious!

Complicated words and sentences will draw attention to "you" rather than God's message. George Soltau once gave an address that captivated a large audience. A preacher approached him after the service and inquired, "What was it that made that address so impressive?" Mr. Soltau replied, "I only used words of one syllable!"

Watch Your Audience

"Thou therefore gird up thy loins, and arise, and speak unto them all that I command thee: be not dismayed at their faces, lest I confound thee before them." (Jeremiah 1:17) The human eye commands authority. The preacher must preach "eye to eye," "face to face," and "heart to heart." Looking at the audience allows you to read their reaction and respond to it. Be ready to respond to that need—conviction, discomfort, emergencies, etc.

Chapter Ten - Character of Preachers

Early in a revival meeting a man wanted to talk about the lack of assurance of salvation that he was experiencing in his life. We talked several times that week, but I couldn't seem to get through. He was faithful in his attendance to church, he drove a Sunday school bus, but he was convinced he could not know for sure that he was on his way to Heaven. Nothing I said seemed to do any good.

Later in that week, I was concluding a message on the cross with an illustration. About half-way through my captivating story, this man stood to his feet and began walking down the aisle just to the right of the pulpit. I happened to be away from the pulpit over on that same side of the platform, and there he was, in front of everyone, standing right in front of me, looking me square in the eye. I stopped, called him by name, and said, "What is it?" He said, "I see it now—it's faith! I need faith! I need to be saved!" I looked at the pastor who was seated with his wife on the front row and said, "Pastor, come and help this man trust Christ." I then looked at the audience and pointed to the two men kneeling at the altar and said, "Here is a man trusting Christ. Who else here tonight needs to come and do the same?" Immediately, six other adults rose to their feet and came to the front to be saved! I never did get to finish my story—but you know what—I really did not care!

Watch Your Time

People consider time to be the most valuable possession they have. Their schedules are busy and there isn't much we can do about that. If the audience is programmed in their minds to give you only so much time to preach—you are going to have to watch your time. The honest truth is we can say a lot in a short amount of time if we properly prepare and discipline ourselves in the pulpit to stick with the message.

One of the best things that ever happened to me was when a pastor informed me that their church had a daily "Dial-A-Devotion." That is, people could call a phone number and they would receive a sixty second message from the church. They had advertised this in the local paper and the response daily was really quite amazing. During the week I was there, the pastor asked me to record these sixty-second messages. He said, "Be sure to let them know about the revival each night, what you will be preaching on, and then make sure that you give a clear presentation of the Gospel!" "Are you kidding?" I asked, "in sixty seconds?" I spent an hour every day preparing that sixty-second message. It was good discipline to make good use of time.

George Elliott once remarked, "Blessed is the man who, having nothing to say, refrains from giving wordy evidence of that fact." Someone else added, "The man who thinks by the inch, and talks by the yard, ought to be dealt with by the foot!" Spurgeon said, "It is a good thing to hit the nail on the head, but don't keep hitting it after it has been driven in, else the wood split and the nail will fall out."

Watch For Results

If God promises to bless His Word, should we not expect results from it being preached? No one would shoot a gun and not look to see if he hit anything! The Gospel must be aimed carefully, and then delivered carefully, and then carefully observed as to its effect. We cannot manufacture results—God must give them. But He does promise, "He that goeth forth and weepeth, bearing precious seed, shall doubtless come again with rejoicing, bringing his sheaves with him." (Psalm 126:6) So look for results and expect them!

A preacher once approached Spurgeon and inquired, "How do you account for the fact that though I preach the same Gospel as you, I do not get anywhere near the same results?" Spurgeon replied, "But you surely don't expect results every time you preach, do you?" "Oh no," answered the man. "Then," Spurgeon explained, "That is one reason why you don't get any."

Conclusion

The ministry is often described as a twenty-four/seven type of "job." By that, it is meant that the preacher is always "on call." When people need you, you must be available regardless of the circumstance. But being a preacher is a twenty-four/seven responsibility "personally" as well. There is no "time off" from being a man of God.

Perhaps some who are reading this have never yet preached a sermon; you are just starting out. Here is a place that you can begin now regardless of your age and training in homiletics. Start with developing a holy character and pure heart for the ministry. Others reading this are veterans of the ministry and your homiletical skills are more than able. But don't neglect this area of your inner heart before God. The title of this book is *Homiletics from the Heart*! I will thus close this chapter with another excerpt from Beecher's lecture at Yale on "Christian Manhood:"

"It is not a small thing to be a minister of Christ. To be a mere priest is a very little thing. In the priestly office there is an appointed round of duties which can be easily performed. But to be a servant of souls; to be Christ's educator of men's interior nature; to stand in the place of the Lord Jesus, not in his majesty of power, but in his spirit, and to attempt to do in your sphere what Christ by his example taught you to do; to know men; to understand their weaknesses; to perceive their sins, and to sympathize with them and sorrow for them on account of their infirmities, and bring the truth so to bear on them as to fill them up, each in the particular spot where he is deficient, and give proportion and harmony to every part; to preach so that sanctification shall be the end of your ministration—this requires an industry, a perseverance, a faith, a self-denial, and an intensity of love, which is demanded by no other profession. If one is a servant of men for Christ's sake and for man's sake, there is nothing that he can aspire to which is so noble as the work which he has chosen. It is the highest calling to which a man can devote himself. And when you return and come to Zion with songs and everlasting joy upon your heads; when out of the heavenly gate come the multitudes whom your ministry has served, to welcome you—in that hour it shall be revealed to you that he who serves the eternities by serving the souls of men and women, is greater than he who builds temples, or paints pictures, or governs empires, or secures to himself all the sweet and desirable things of earth."[56]

Chapter Eleven - Controlled By The Holy Spirit   127

pastor called and asked if we would be willing to conduct a Vacation Bible School in the morning hours as well as preach the revival meeting at night. He said that they had not had a VBS for years and felt that it would be a help. I had preached quite often to children and my wife had taught children's meetings as well and so I said, "Sure—no problem."

I knew the church was not large and so my wife and I began to work on a program for the week that we could basically conduct ourselves. She would teach some stories and I would lead the song service and preach the main message. I just assumed the church would have some lay folks that would help out with a craft, refreshments, and break time.

When we arrived at the church on Saturday evening, we found a small building that would seat about fifty comfortably. The church was running thirty in attendance, but outside of the pastor's family, there was no one in the church much under 60 years of age! The church could not support the pastor financially and so he was working a full-time job and would not be available in the mornings for Bible School. I preached Sunday to thirty folks who were very kind and sweet. But there were no children!

That afternoon, I drove around the little town and noticed children everywhere. As I observed them closely, I noticed that many of them were Spanish-speaking children. As I enquired about this, I discovered that this little town was located in the heart of a very fertile valley known for its vegetable farming. Del Monte, Jolly Green Giant, and other companies had huge factories there and many of these Spanish-speaking people had come there for the summer to work in the fields and factories harvesting and canning these vegetables.

I noticed that the church had an old bus and so I asked if it was in working condition. The pastor assured me that it was and gave us permission to take it out the next morning and pick up children. You can get children excited about anything, and we had a time each day filling that old bus up and conducting Bible School. We averaged over a hundred in that little building each day, and as I recall there were over fifty boys and girls saved. Each night we would have the same thirty adults for the evening revival service.

About Wednesday, I had a brainstorm. I said, "Pastor, every Vacation Bible School has a program at the end of the week. Why don't we have a program on Friday night and see if we can get the parents of these children to come to the revival meeting?" He thought it was an excellent idea. I ran off some flyers and the next day promoted the program. As I said, children get excited easily and they responded wonderfully as I told them that on Friday night at 7:00 p.m. we would be singing our songs and saying our verses to their parents and friends. I encouraged them to bring everyone they could.

Seven o'clock came on Friday night and that little building was packed! There were people sitting on the floor, in the window sills, and standing across the back. Seventy-five children had come back for the program and there were at least that many adults stuffed into that tiny, un-air-conditioned building. I was a nervous wreck fearing that the children would not do well and mess up the service. (You never know what children are going to do during a program—throw up, faint, wave to the crowd—you name it—it is possible!) But they were amazing! The program went very well and the children all took their seats as now I was going to preach the Gospel for the next thirty minutes.

When children perform, they get very tense and when it is over, they relax. Not more than five minutes into my message, with the children all relaxed and sitting on the left side of the auditorium, it seemed that every one of them suddenly needed to use the restroom. One by one they got up and made their way down the rickety stairway to the basement where there was just one bathroom for both genders. Five minutes later, it seemed as though every child was either on their way down or on their way up that stairway. I thought about stopping them, but I feared a world-wide flood!

I decided to ignore them and concentrate on preaching to the adults on the right side of the auditorium After all, the message was designed for them. As I preached, these people, many of whom were Spanish-speaking, began to converse out loud with each other in Spanish. I had no idea what they were saying and so simply tried to raise the volume of my voice and out preach them. On the very back row of the church, an old drunk had stumbled in and sat down. About half way through my message, he stood up and drawled, "I've had enough of this—I'm getting out of here!" With that he headed for the door, tripped over the threshold and tumbled down the four or five steps and landed in a heap on the sidewalk in front of the church, groaning as he did. One of the deacons quickly slipped out, helped him up, and brought him back in!

Now, I have seventy-five kids going to the restroom, I have people talking out loud in Spanish, and I have a drunk in the back yelling, "This guy's crazy—I don't know why we're listening to him!" I was boiling! I had created a monster and there was no way out. Preaching in my flesh, I began to race through the rest of the sermon as fast as I could. I didn't care any more—I just wanted to get out of there and go home!

I ended the message and asked everyone to close their eyes. (None of the Spanish folks did until I demonstrated it by putting my hands over my eyes and yelling at them to CLOSE THEIR EYES!!) Without any concern in my voice, I rudely said, (because this is what you are supposed to say after you preach), "If you are here tonight and on your way to Hell, raise your hand and I will pray for you!" (I had just preached a message on the subject of Hell. There was a time when I thought we might be experiencing a little of it right then.) I had no more than asked the question, when five men's hands shot straight up in the air. I said, "No, place your hand down—you did not understand the question!" With a little more concern, however, in my voice, I said, "If you are here tonight and not sure that you would go to Heaven if you died, please raise your hand, and I will pray for you." Those same five men raised their hands.

Suddenly, in my heart, I was hearing the sweet voice of the Spirit of God saying, Son, "Not by might, nor by power, but by my spirit, saith the Lord of hosts." (Zechariah 4:6) When I gave the invitation that evening, those five men came on the first stanza and many others followed them to the altar to be saved. I had done everything wrong, but somehow the engine got turned on! "It is the spirit that quickeneth; the flesh profiteth nothing: the words that I speak unto you, they are spirit, and they are life." (John 6:63)

The Gift Of The Holy Spirit

Just what is it that the Holy Spirit does for us? The following is by no means exhaustive and not intended to be. Rather, I only want you to see how foolish it is for us to attempt to "Preach the Word" without Him who empowers it all!

He Is The Spirit Of Knowledge

"Howbeit when he, the Spirit of truth, is come, he will guide you into all truth..." (John 16:13) If we are not first taught by Him, how can we expect to teach others? We need His help a whole lot more than the commentators or computer programs. "Open thou mine eyes, that I may behold wondrous things out of thy law. I am a stranger in the earth: hide not thy commandments from me." (Psalm 119:18-19)

The Holy Spirit is especially given to show us knowledge concerning Christ. "...for he shall not speak of himself; ... He shall glorify me: for he shall receive of mine, and shall shew it unto you." (John 16:13-14) And since, "...we preach not ourselves, but Christ Jesus the Lord..." (II Corinthians 4:5), we need Him to instruct us in "the knowledge of our Lord and Saviour Jesus Christ." (II Peter 3:18)

Spurgeon said, "Since He especially delights in the things of Christ, and focuses His sacred light upon the cross, we rejoice to see the center of our testimony so divinely illuminated, and we are sure that the light will be diffused over all the rest of our ministry."[57]

He Is The Spirit of Wisdom

Knowledge can be dangerous without wisdom—"Knowledge puffeth up... ." (I Corinthians 8:1) Wisdom is the art of rightly using what we know. "...rightly dividing the word of truth." (II Timothy 2:15) We must have wisdom to preach the whole counsel of God but making sure that we are doing so in the right season—"To everything there is a season, and a time for every purpose under the heaven." (Ecclesiastes 3:1)

Someone has said, "You can lead a horse to water, but you can't make him drink." To which another has added, "True, but you can put salt in his oats to make him thirsty." We need to have the Spirit's wisdom to enable us to "put salt in the oats" so that people will come and "take the water of life freely." (Revelation 22:17)

He Is The Spirit Of Utterance
Paul asked the Ephesian church, "Praying always with all prayer and supplication in the Spirit... And for me, that utterance may be given unto me, that I may open my mouth boldly, to make known the mystery of the gospel." (Ephesians 6:18-19) We need knowledge to know "what" to preach, and wisdom to know "how," but oh, how we need utterance that will "enable" us to do so with power and freedom! Again, Paul asked in II Thessalonians 3:1, "Finally, brethren, pray for us, that the word of the Lord may have free course, and be glorified, even as it is with you:"

He Is The Spirit Of Anointing
He is the oil that permeates our entire being as a preacher. It is with this anointing that Paul came to Corinth to preach: "And I, brethren, when I came to you, came not with excellency of speech or of wisdom, declaring unto you the testimony of God. For I determined not to know any thing among you, save Jesus Christ, and him crucified. And I was with you in weakness, and in fear, and in much trembling. And my speech and my preaching was not with enticing

words of man's wisdom, but in demonstration of the Spirit and of power: That your faith should not stand in the wisdom of men, but in the power of God." (I Corinthians 2:1-5)

"Especially is it the Holy Spirit's work to maintain in us a devotional frame of mind whilst we are discoursing. This is a condition to be greatly coveted—to continue praying while you are occupied with preaching; to do the Lord's commandments, hearkening unto the voice of His word; to keep the eye on the throne, and the wing in perpetual motion. I hope we know what this means; I am sure we know, or may soon experience, its opposite, namely, the evil of preaching in an undevotional spirit. What can be worse than to speak under the influence of a proud or angry spirit? What is more weakening than to preach in an unbelieving spirit? But, oh, to burn in our secret heart while we blaze before the eyes of others! This is the work of the Spirit of God. Work it in us, O adorable Comforter!"[58]

He Is The Spirit Of Fruit
Nothing eternal is accomplished apart from the work of the Holy Spirit. There is no fruit apart from His fruit. "Who also hath made us able ministers of the new testament; not of the letter, but of the spirit: for the letter killeth, but the spirit giveth life." (II Corinthians 3:6) We are just tools in His hand, but tools when yielded to His control can be used to gather a great harvest of fruit.

The Grieving Of The Holy Spirit

The Holy Spirit's power is an absolute essential to the preacher of God's Word. Since we are commanded to "...be filled with the Spirit" (Ephesians 5:18), it is obvious that it is possible to be "empty of the Spirit." Spurgeon states, "Let none of us try the experiment, but it is certain that ministers may lose the aid of the Holy Ghost. Each man here may lose it. You shall not perish as believers, for everlasting life is in you; but you may perish as ministers, and be no more heard of as witnesses for the Lord. Should this happen it will not be without a cause. The Spirit claims a sovereignty like that of the wind which bloweth where it listeth; but let us never dream that sovereignty and capriciousness are the same thing. The blessed Spirit acts as He wills, but He always acts justly, wisely, and with motive and reason. At times He gives or withholds His blessing, for reasons connected with ourselves... The Spirit of God may be grieved and vexed and even resisted: To deny this is to oppose the constant testimony of Scripture. Worst of all, we may do despite to Him, and so insult Him that He will speak no more by us, but leave us as He left King Saul of old... . 'Tell it not in Gath, publish it not in the streets of Askelon; lest the daughters of the Philistines rejoice, lest the daughters of the uncircumcised triumph. How are the mighty fallen in the midst of the battle!'" (II Samuel 1:20, 25)[59]

He Is Grieved By Our Insensitivity

Too often we minister without an ear to Him. We rely upon our experience, understanding, and training rather than the impulse of the Spirit of God. "Turn you at my reproof: behold, I will pour out my spirit unto you, I will make known my words unto you. Because I have called, and ye refused; I have stretched out my hand, and no man regarded; But ye have set at nought all my counsel, and would none of my reproof." (Proverbs 1:23-25)

He Is Grieved By Our Dishonesty

When a musician begins to play the violin and finds it out of tune, he immediately stops and adjusts the instrument so that the notes are true. God cannot use a "double-minded" preacher—he is unstable and unfit for service. Paul asks, "Thou therefore which teachest another, teachest thou not thyself? thou that preachest a man should not steal, dost thou steal? Thou that sayest a man should not commit adultery, dost thou commit adultery? thou that abhorrest idols, dost thou commit sacrilege? Thou that makest thy boast of the law, through breaking the law dishonourest thou God? For the name of God is blasphemed among the Gentiles through you... ." (Romans 2:21-24)

He Is Grieved By Pride

The fastest way to drive away the Spirit of God from your ministry is through pride. "Though the Lord be high, yet hath he respect unto the lowly: but the proud he knoweth afar off." (Psalm 138:6) Lucifer lost his position through pride (Isaiah 14:12-16); Nebuchadnezzar lost his kingdom (Daniel 5:18-21); King Herod lost his life (Acts 12:21-23). God can't use what He hates: "These six things doth the Lord hate: yea, seven are an abomination unto him: A proud look... ." (Proverbs 6:16-17)

He Is Grieved By Laziness

The Holy Spirit will not lie at the door of the sluggard and supply the deficiencies caused by laziness. The Spirit of God is constantly "working" in lives and he is much pleased to have a vessel through which He can work. "That ye be not slothful, but followers of them who through faith and patience inherit the promises." (Hebrews 6:12)

He Is Grieved By Prayerlessness
"...ye have not, because ye ask not." (James 3:2) "What, could ye not watch with me one hour? ... the spirit indeed is willing, but the flesh is weak." (Matthew 26:40-41) When we don't pray we are telling the Holy Spirit, we will do the work without Him. We do not need Him—we can handle it ourselves.

Conclusion

In Luke 11:13, Jesus said: "If ye then, being evil, know how to give good gifts unto your children: how much more shall your heavenly Father give the Holy Spirit to them that ask him?" The key to powerful, effective preaching is already in the ignition. We can choose to push the car ourselves, or we can engage his power. It is our choice!

Perry Downs states, "The content of Scripture taught in the power of the Holy Spirit does change lives. God can use our (preaching) to change lives... . There must be a supernatural intervention in our ministry for lives to be touched... . We are able to entertain, enlighten, teach, and lead people, but to enable a person to grow in faith requires a touch from God... . It is a spiritual battle. We dare not trivialize the work by creating silly gimmicks... rather, we must understand that we are dependent on His Spirit... . It is God who must give a new heart (Ezekiel 36:24-32), and God who brings his own to maturity."[60]

"O, for the Spirit of God to make and keep us alive unto God, faithful to our office, and useful to our generation, and clear of the blood of men's souls."[61]

Conclusion

As I sit down to type my final thoughts, my dad's life hangs in the balance. The doctors say it could be hours, maybe days, but, of course, life is in the hands of the Lord. I have thought of him often as I have written these chapters. I have learned a lot about "homiletics" from some great teachers, from some great books, and from listening to some outstanding preachers, but I have learned about the "heart" from my dad.

As I stated earlier, I am not a PK (preacher's kid), my dad was a dairy farmer, as was my grandfather, and my great grandfather. The only time I ever saw my dad behind a pulpit was, as chairman of the deacons, he gave the pastor his Christmas gift. My dad did not sing in the choir or teach a

Sunday school class. Most people in the church knew about Marvin Goetsch (he was a deacon for over 40 years), but I doubt that many people really knew him. He was quiet, humble, unassuming, but always faithful.

Dad was saved in a six-week long revival meeting in 1930 at the age of nine. His dad drove the family the seven miles to church each night in a Model A Ford. I do not remember my dad ever missing church, a deacon's meeting, a revival or a mission's conference. Dad and Mom cleaned the church every Saturday, and my older sister and my younger brother and I always went along and helped with something. It was a way of life—being faithful—serving. That is what I mean about the "heart."

I never heard my dad and mom quarrel or raise their voice at each other. I remember at least twice a guest preacher speaking about the home and asking the crowd if there was anyone there who had never had a fight with his wife? My dad's hand would get about half way up, when the preacher would say, "If you raise your hand to that, you are a liar," and my dad would quietly lower his hand—but he was not lying!

I have never known a man more tender hearted than my dad. He would cry when you did wrong and when you did right. I remember when I was in junior high, I came home from ball practice after Dad had already gone to the barn to start the milking. Mom was finishing up the kitchen chores and as I sat down to eat my supper, Mom sensed that I was in trouble at school (woman's intuition), I guess. After scolding me severely, she grabbed me by the arm, bent me over, and began to spank me! I was a junior higher and thought I was pretty tough, but she was hurting me! There was no way I was going to let her know that though, and so when she finished, I stood up, looked at her, and shrugged my shoulders as if to say, is that the best you can do? She pointed outside and said, "You go see your dad!"

The barn was about one hundred yards from the house, and I took my good-natured time getting there. I knew which end of the barn my dad would be on, and so I quietly entered the barn from the opposite end. I slipped in quietly and noticed him down between the cows at the far end, holding a milker on a cow. I walked to where he was, thinking he was unaware of my presence. His back was to me as he crouched down next to the cow. I waited. (I was told as a boy, never to bother my dad when he was working—wait until he is finished. That night I didn't care if he never stopped working. I was in trouble and my mom had already called him on the phone and told him all about it.)

With his back still toward me, he pulled the milker off of the cow and stood up to pull the suction hoses off the air-line. He then picked up the milker full of milk, turned around, stepped over the gutter, and set the can of milk down at my feet. By this time tears were streaming down his face. His lower lip began to quiver and he said, "John, your sin makes me so sick." As he stood there and wept over my sin, I wished that he would just grab me and throw me against the wall, or take a two by four and hit me with it. But he did nothing but weep. He never punished me that night or said another word, but it was those tears that kept me out of a lot of sin through my teen years. I wanted to go to the parties after games with my friends, but I always headed for home, because I never wanted to see those tears again.

Whenever I would preach, and my dad was in the audience, my wife hated to sit near him because he always cried through the message. That's what I mean about the "heart."

I never once heard my dad complain about anything. Oh, he had reason to many times. When he was a young teenager, every one of his teeth abscessed at once and had to be pulled in one day—without any pain-killers! Later on, he was playing some pick-up football and tore the ligaments in both of his knees. He crawled home but never saw a doctor. My dad never played catch or shot hoops with me. He was unable to jump or run or play ball because of the constant severe pain in those knees. Other than the fact that he took two aspirin after every meal, I never knew he hurt until 1985 when he was unable to walk on those crippled legs any longer. When the doctors did surgery to replace his knees, they said there was nothing left but pieces.

Shortly after those knee surgeries he developed a blood clot on his spine, and most of his muscles in his back had to be cut in order to have access to the clot. He was left paralyzed, and doctors said he would never walk again. But by the grace of God, and through a determined "German" will, two years later he was walking and driving a car. That is what I mean about "heart."

In recent years and days, he's fought through congestive heart failure, pneumonia, strokes, blindness, an obstructed bowel, to name just the major battles. When I saw him last, I watched him struggle for nearly an hour to just stand up on his feet so that he could move from his chair to a wheelchair. With perspiration on his brow and his body aching and exhausted, there was no word of complaint—not even a groan! That's what I mean about "heart."

When I left him, my mom told him it would be a few weeks before I could return. He looked at me and said, "Okay, I will be looking for you"—and whether I see him again in this life or have to wait until Heaven—I know he will. Today, in a hospital bed, he battles on—undaunted in his love for his family, his church, and his God. That is what I mean about the "heart."

I do not guess I could have learned that part of the ministry from anyone else. My dad never taught me anything about declarations, propositions, transitional sentences, delivery, or how to tell an illustration, but he taught me everything about "doing the will of God from the heart" (Ephesians 6:6).

And that is why this has not just been a textbook about homiletics. Lots of preachers could write that better than I could. This has been about "Homiletics from the Heart" because Preacher, if your heart is not in the ministry—you will not make it. It is too tough, painful, and exhausting to do just to make a living. Every time you pray, prepare a sermon, go soulwinning, counsel, or preach a sermon, you are in an all-out war with the prince and power of the air! The homiletics part will not get you through this battle, you will drop the sword and run for tents of ease. But if your heart is in this thing—your hand will cleave to the sword, and you will fight to the end.

No doubt, soon, the Captain of the host, will call Marvin David Goetsch home from the battle. He will be retired from active earthly duty and will be re-assigned to the heavenly ranks. Someone will need to take his place.

This world needs more good preachers and I hope these chapters have helped you in some way to be a more effective preacher of the Word. But before we can develop into good preachers, we've got to be good Christians! I'll be honest, I've learned more from my dad's life as a Christian than I have learned from all the sermons I've ever heard!

Somehow, I think if we could get the "heart" part, the "homiletics" part would be a lot easier, and the result would be revival in the pulpit and in the pew.

Conclusion

"Just One Sermon"
A Tribute to Marvin D. Goetsch
May 29, 1921—January 18, 2003

He never preached from a pulpit—this man I called Dad,
But he was the best example of Jesus Christ a kid could have had.
His life never wavered in good times or in pain,
His character was blameless even when life began to wane.
He was like a Rock of Gibralter: consistent, faithful, and true,
Though others were more prominent—Dad was the
best Christian I knew.

He taught me how to work, rising early to the task,
"What time would he get up?"—you never had to ask.
Those farming days were long, and a chance to play was slim,
But it never really mattered because I was content to be with him.
Everything he was, I wanted in me, to be the same,
I was glad he was my dad and proud to bear his name.

His words were often few, but his life spoke loud and clear,
And you knew what was important when his
eyes would fill with tears.
He loved his family, his church, his Bible, and his God,
"Faithful" could sum up his journey on earth's sod.
His trials taught him patience and to listen to God's voice,
"The will of God," for him and us—there was no other choice.

For him, today, life's burdens are all past,
There is no pain or suffering in his mansion now at last.
No, he never preached, or taught a class, or sang in choirs great,
His name remains unknown to the rich and heads of state.
But from his life, a single sermon came,
with no points but just this one:
Live each day in such a way, that you'll hear
those words—"Well Done."

– John Goetsch

*My dad went home to be with the Lord less than two weeks after this book was completed. The above poem was written the day he died and I had the privilege of reading it at his funeral on January 21, 2003.

Appendix 1

The Putting Off—Putting On Principle

The preaching of the Word of God is both negative and positive. Paul tells us in II Timothy 3:16 that all Scripture is given by inspiration of God and is profitable for:

*Doctrine: That is what is **right**.*
*Reproof: That is what is **wrong**.*
*Correction: That is **how to get right**.*
*Instruction in righteousness: That is **how to stay right**.*

Thus, when we "preach the Word" both right and wrong are going to be revealed. The truth is—most people already know when things are wrong in their lives. God's Word has been "...written in their hearts, their conscience also bearing witness... ." (Romans 2:15) The preaching of God's Word exposes the error in people's lives and causes them to change their mind about that sin and repent. Often, that is what the invitation is all about—confessing sin and getting right with God.

However, we must go a step further, because the Bible does. If all we do is empty our life of sin, we leave a void for the devil to fill with something else. "When the unclean spirit is gone out of a man, he walketh through dry places, seeking rest, and findeth none. Then he saith, I will return into my house from when I came out; and when he is come, he findeth it empty, swept, and garnished. Then goeth he, and taketh with himself seven other spirits more wicked than himself, and they enter in and dwell there: and the last state of that man is worse than the first. Even so shall it be also unto this wicked generation." (Matthew 12:43-45)

The "old" must be replaced with "new" or it will be replaced by worse "old." Notice carefully this principle in Paul's instruction in Ephesians 4: "But ye have not so learned Christ; If so be that ye have heard him, and have been taught by him, as the truth is in Jesus: That ye put off concerning the former conversation the old man, which is corrupt according to the deceitful lusts; And be renewed in the spirit of your mind; And that ye put on the new man, which after God is created in righteousness and true holiness. Wherefore putting away lying, speak every man truth with his neighbour: for we are members one of another. Be ye angry, and sin not: let not the sun go down upon your wrath: Neither give place to the devil. Let him that stole steal no more: but rather let him labour, working with his hands the thing which is good, that he may have to give to him that needeth. Let no corrupt communication proceed out of your mouth, but that which is good to the use of edifying, that it may minister grace unto the hearers. And grieve not the Holy Spirit of God, whereby ye are sealed unto the day of redemption. Let all bitterness, and wrath, and anger, and clamour, and evil speaking, be put away from you with all malice: And be ye kind one to another, tenderhearted, forgiving one another, even as God for Christ's sake hath forgiven you." (verses 20-32)

As Paul deals with certain sins, he not only instructs the believers to put them off, but then specifically states what should be put there in its place. For Christian growth and maturity to take place "dehabitation"—that is, breaking the old habits of sin, and "rehabitation"—that is, establishing the new patterns of thinking and living must occur.

Someone has said, "You can't teach an old dog new tricks." Well, first of all we are not talking about "dogs"—we are talking about "people." Secondly, we are not talking about "tricks"—we are talking about "holy living by the grace of God." Either we believe the Bible or we do not! God is in the business of "changing lives." He changes us at conversion and makes us a brand new creature (II Corinthians 5:17), and then changes us continually through the process of sanctification (II Corinthians 3:18). "There hath no temptation taken you but such as is common to man: but God is faithful, who will not suffer you to be tempted above that ye are able; but will with the temptation also make a way to escape, that ye may be able to bear it." (I Corinthians 10:13)

The Bible is filled with "instead ofs." For example, in James 5:12 it says, "But above all things, my brethren, swear not, neither by heaven, neither by the earth, neither by any other oath: but let your yea be yea; and your nay, nay; lest ye fall into condemnation." What about Psalm 1:1-2? "Blessed is the man that walketh not in the counsel of the ungodly, nor standeth in the way of sinners, nor sitteth in the seat of the scornful. But his delight is in the law of the Lord; and in his law doth he meditate day and night." The wrong action—the wrong habit, being replaced by the right action—the right habit!

Listen to James, "Submit yourselves therefore to God. Resist the devil, and he will flee from you. Draw nigh to God, and he will draw nigh to you. Cleanse your hands, ye sinners; and purify your hearts, ye double minded. Be afflicted, and mourn, and weep: let your laughter be turned to mourning, and your joy to heaviness. Humble yourselves in the sight of the Lord, and he shall lift you up." (James 4: 7-10) Or how about Ephesians 5:18? "And be not drunk with wine, wherein is excess; but be filled with the spirit;"

There is no such thing as "instant holiness." "Enoch walked with God." (Genesis 5:24) "So Jotham became mighty, because he prepared his ways before the Lord his God." (II Chronicles 27:6) Paul instructed Timothy to "exercise thyself rather unto godliness." (I Timothy 4:7) Spiritual maturity is an on-going process of replacing the old with the new. Enoch did not get from point A to point B in one step—he walked with God. "...If any man will come after me, let him deny himself, and take up his cross daily, and follow me." (Luke 9:23)

Thus, as we "preach the Word," we must expose the old and explain the new. We must preach repentance, but also replacement. Denying the old, and dedication to the new. Forsaking sin and following the Saviour. Starving the flesh, and saturating ourselves with the Spirit. As we feed the flock of God, we must serve a "balanced" diet if they are going to be healthy sheep.

Listed below are 82 common sins that need to be "put off" from our lives and their counterparts that should be "put on" in their place. With each of these "old" and "new" habits we have listed several verses that reinforce the principle. These are great verses for people to memorize who are struggling with these areas. Jesus confronted the temptations of Satan with Scripture and we are wise to take the "sword of the Spirit, which is the Word of God" and do likewise. As we preach and counsel people—let's not just "rebuke" the sin, but let's help people "replace" that old habit with a new one.

"Put Off"

1. Lack of Love
   I Thess. 3:12; I John 4:7,8,20

2. Judging
   I Cor. 4:5; Rom. 14:4; James 4:12; Matthew 7:1-5

3. Bitterness
   *James 3:14-15; Eph. 4:31
   Heb. 12:15*

4. Unforgiving spirit
   Matt. 6:14; Mark 11:25-26

"Put On"

1. Love
   *John 15:12; John 13:35
   I Peter 1:22*

2. Search my own sin
   *John 8:9; John 15:22
   Psalm 139:23-24;
   Jer. 17:10*

3. Tenderheartedness
   *Col. 3:12; Rom. 12:10
   II Peter 1:5-7*

4. Forgiving spirit
   *Matt. 6:14; Luke 17:4
   Col. 3:13*

5. Pride
   Prov. 11:2; Prov. 21:4; Prov. 28:25; Prov. 16:18

5. Humility
   James 4:6; Prov. 16:19 Prov. 22:4; Prov. 29:23 Matt. 18:4

6. Selfishness
   Isaiah 5:8; Matt. 25:43 Phil. 2:21

6. Death to self
   John 12:24; Matt. 16:25 I Cor. 10:24; Phil. 2:4 Gal. 2:20

7. Boasting (conceit)
   Gal. 6:3; Prov. 17:19; Prov. 25:6-7; I Cor. 4:7

7. Humility
   Prov. 27:2; Matt. 23:12 I Pet. 5:5-6

8. Stubbornness
   II Chron. 24:19; Acts 7:51 I Sam. 15:23

8. Submission
   Rom. 6:13; Matt. 6:10 Matt. 26:39

9. Lack of Submission
   II Peter 2:10; Eph. 6:6 II Tim. 3:6

9. Broken will
   Matt. 6:10; Psalm 40:8 Matt. 12:50

10. Rebellion
    Jer. 44:16; Zech. 7:11 I Sam. 15:23

10. Submission
    Joel 2:12-13; Luke 1:38 James 4:7

11. Disobedience
    Eph. 5:6; II Thess. 1:8 Heb. 2:2-3

11. Obedience
    Heb. 5:9; Deut. 26:16 I Sam. 15:22; Acts 5:29

12. Ungratefulness
    Luke 17:17-18; Deut. 32:6 Rom 1:21

12. Thankfulness
    Eph. 5:20; Deut. 8:10 Psalm 100:4; Col. 3:15

13. Impatience
    Ecc. 7:8; Psalm 40:1
    James 1:2-4

14. Discontentment
    Prov. 15:16; Deut. 32:32
    Phil. 4:11-12

15. Covetousness
    Jer. 6:13; Hab. 2:9; Luke 12:15
    Exodus 20:17

16. Murmuring
    John 6:43; Phil. 2:14; Prov. 19:3

17. Complaining
    Psalm 77:3; Jude 15-16

18. Sassing
    Isaiah 57:4; John 6:43

19. Irritation to others
    Prov. 17:14; Prov. 26:17
    Prov. 25:8

20. Jealousy
    Gen. 37:4; Prov. 27:4

21. Strife
    Prov. 3:30; Prov. 20:3
    James 3:16

13. Patience
    Luke 21:19; Rom. 12:12
    Heb. 10:36; James 1:4
    James 5:7

14. Satisfaction
    Heb. 13:5; I Tim. 6:6

15. Yielded rights
    Col. 3:5; Rom. 13:14
    Gal. 5:16

16. Gratefulness
    I Cor. 10:10; I Thess 5:18

17. Contentment
    Heb. 13:5; Psalm 142:4

18. Respect for authority
    Eph. 5:21; Heb. 13:17
    I Cor. 16:16

19. Preferring in love
    Phil. 2:3-4; II Tim. 2:14

20. Trust
    I Cor. 13:4; Prov. 3:5-6

21. Esteeming others
    Luke 6:31; Mark 12:31
    Rom. 13:10; Rom. 15:1,2
    Gal. 5:14

22. Losing temper *Prov. 14:17; Prov. 16:32*	22. Self control *Rom. 5:3–4; Prov. 19:11*
23. Bodily harm *Acts 16:28; Prov. 16:29*	23. Gentleness *I Thess. 2:7; II Tim. 2:4* *James 3:17*
24. Anger *Ecc. 7:9; Prov. 14:17*	24. Self control *Gal. 5:24–25; I Cor. 9:25*
25. Wrath *Psalm 37:8; James 1:19–20*	25. Self control *Gal. 5:24–25; Rom. 6:12*
26. Hatred *Matt. 5:21–22*	26. Kindness *I Cor. 13:3; Matt. 22:39*
27. Murder *Matt. 19:18; Rom. 13:9* *Ex. 20:13*	27. Love *Rom. 13:10; I Peter 1:22*
28. Gossip *Titus 3:2; James 3:6* *James 4:11*	28. Speaking with praise *Rom. 14:19; Eph. 4:12* *Eph. 4:29*
29. Lying *Prov. 12:19; Psalm 5:6* *Psalm 101:7; Prov. 12:22* *Col. 3:9*	29. Speaking truth *Zech. 8:16; Eph. 6:14*
30. Bad language *Eph. 4:31; Eph. 4:29*	30. Edifying *I Tim. 4:12; Prov. 16:14* *Col. 4:6*
31. Profanity *Ecc. 10:12; Psalm 109:17*	31. Edifying *I Tim. 4:12; Prov. 25:11*

32. Idle words
    I Tim. 6:3-4; Matt. 12:36

33. Evil thoughts
    I Chron. 28:9; Prov. 15:26
    Prov. 23:7

34. Bad motives
    Prov. 6:18; Rom. 1:21
    Psalm 38:12; Gen. 11:6

35. Complacency
    Rev. 3:15; James 4:17

36. Hypocrisy
    Matt. 23:23-25; Isaiah 29:13
    Job 8:13

37. Other gods
    Josh. 24:14-15; Deut. 11:16

38. Loss of first love
    Hosea 10:2; Matt. 24:12
    Rev. 2:4

39. Lack of rejoicing
    Psalm 85:6; Phil. 4:4

40. Worry
    Matt. 6:25-34

32. Bridled tongue
    Prov. 21:23; James 3:2-3

33. Good thoughts
    Phil. 4:8; Rom. 8:6
    Phil. 2:5

34. Meditation
    Psalm 19:14; Psalm 119:59; Prov. 12:5

35. Diligence
    Col. 3:23; Deut. 6:5
    Psalm 119:2; Jer. 29:13
    Ecc. 9:10

36. Honesty
    Eph. 4:25; Luke 6:46
    Rom. 2:21; James 3:10

37. Christ in first place
    Eph. 4:6; Matt. 6:33
    Acts 3:26

38. Meditation on Christ's love
    I John 4:10,19

39. Rejoicing
    I Thess. 5:16; I Peter 1:8

40. Trust
    I Peter 5:7; Phil. 4:6

41. Doubt
   Luke 18:8; I John 5:4
   I Thess. 5:24

42. Unfaithfulness
   Prov. 20:6; Prov. 25:19
   I Cor. 4:2

43. Copping out
   Prov. 24:10; Matt. 24:26

44. Neglect of Bible study
   Psalm 119:9-11; II Tim.
   3:14-17

45. Neglect of prayer
   Luke 18:1; Eph. 6:18
   I Chron. 16:11

46. No soulwinning
   Ezekiel 33:8-9

47. Burying talents
   Matt. 25:14-30

48. Irresponsibility
   Prov. 24:30-34

49. Procrastination
   James 4:13-15; Prov. 27:1

41. Faith
   Heb. 11:1; Luke 17:5

42. Faithfulness
   Psalm 31:23; Rev. 2:10
   Luke 19:17

43. Discipline
   Luke 14:27; I Cor. 9:
   24-27

44. Devotions
   Josh. 1:8; Isaiah 34:16
   I Tim. 2:15

45. Prayer
   Psalm 55:17; Heb. 4:16
   Mark 1:35; II Chron.
   7:14

46. Soulwinning
   Prov. 11:30; Dan. 12:3
   James 5:20; Matt. 4:19
   Jude 22-23

47. Perfecting abilities
   Luke 12:48; I Cor. 4:2

48. Responsibility
   Eph. 4:1; Prov. 6:6-11

49. Discipline
   John 9:4; Psalm 95:7-8

50. Laziness
Prov. 13:4; Prov. 20:4
Prov. 21:25; Eph. 5:15-16

51. Not doing your best
Prov. 14:23; Ecc. 9:10

52. Misconduct in church
I Tim. 3:15; Psalm 122:1

53. No tithing
Mal. 3:7-10

54. Inhospitable
I Peter 4:9

55. Temporal values
Phil. 3:8; Hag. 1:5-7
Prov. 13:7; Matt. 6:19-21

56. Following the crowd
Prov. 29:25-26; I Cor. 15:33
Psalm 1:1; Prov. 4:14
Ex. 34:12

57. Cheating
I Peter 2:12; Prov. 15:3

58. Stealing
Ex. 20:15; I Peter 4:15
Eph. 4:28

59. Lack of moderation
Col. 3:13; Phil. 4:5

50. Diligence
I Cor. 10:31; Prov. 22:29
II Peter 3:14

51. Doing your best
Col. 3:23; I Cor. 14:12

52. Reverence
Ecc. 5:1; Psalm 26:8
Psalm 27:4

53. Tithing
I Cor. 9:6-7; 16:1-2

54. Hospitable
Rom. 12:13; Heb. 13:2

55. Eternal values
II Tim. 2:4; Col. 3:2
I Tim. 6:19

56. Following Christ
Matt. 6:33; Isaiah 55:6
Acts 17:27

57. Honesty
Luke 8:15; Rom. 12:17

58. Giving
Luke 6:38; Prov. 3:9-10

59. Balance
II Peter 1:5-10

60. Over-eating
    Prov. 23:21; Prov. 23:1-2

61. Speeding
    I Peter 2:13-14

62. Improper dating relationships
    Gen. 39:9; I Cor. 15:33

63. Dating the wrong people
    II Cor. 6:14

64. Lust of the flesh
    Gal. 5:24; Rom. 6:6
    I John 2:16

65. Lust of the eyes
    Psalm 101:3; I John 2:16

66. Fornication
    I Thess. 4:3-8

67. Necking / Petting
    Prov. 5:20; I Cor. 7:1

68. Immodest dress
    Prov. 11:22

69. Adultery
    Matt. 5:27-28

70. Homosexuality
    Rom. 1:26-27

60. Self control
    I Cor. 9:27; Luke 21:34
    Luke 12:22

61. Obedience to civil law
    Ecc. 8:2; Rom. 13:1

62. God's standards
    Phil. 1:20; I Cor. 6:19,20

63. Equal yoke
    I Cor. 6:12; Amos 3:3

64. Pure desires
    I Peter 2:11; Rom. 13:14
    Col. 3:5

65. Pure thoughts
    Phil. 2:4; I Tim. 5:22

66. Purity
    I Cor. 10:8; Matt. 5:8
    Psalm 24:3-4

67. Abstinence
    I Thess. 4:4; Heb. 13:4

68. Modesty
    I Tim. 2:9

69. Fidelity
    Ex. 20:14; Prov. 5:18

70. God's purpose
    I Tim. 5:22; Gen. 2:24

71. Worldly hair styles
    Phil. 1:27

72. Worldly music
    Psalm 95:1; I Cor. 14:15
    Prov. 23:7

73. Dancing
    I Thess. 5:22

74. Drugs
    Rev. 21:8

75. Drinking
    Prov. 20:1; Isaiah 5:11
    Rom. 13:13; Prov. 23:20

76. Smoking
    I Cor. 6:19-20

77. Witchcraft/Astrology
    Deut. 18:10-11

78. Gambling
    Luke 15:13

79. Movies
    Matt. 6:22-23; Prov. 23:7

80. Stumbling block to others
    I Cor. 8:9-12

81. Preferential treatment
    James 2:1-6

82. Presumption of the future
    James 4:13-14

---

71. Glorifying God
    I Cor. 11:14-15

72. Edifying music
    Eph. 5:19; Col. 3:16

73. Glorifying God
    I Cor. 10:31

74. God's Temple
    I Cor. 3:16-17

75. God's Temple
    Prov. 23:29-35

76. God's Temple
    I Cor. 3:16-17

77. One true God
    Micah 5:12-15

78. Stewardship
    I Cor. 4:2

79. Example
    Psalm 101:3

80. Stepping stone
    Rom. 14:21; Rom. 15:1

81. Fairness
    Luke 6:31; I Tim. 5:21

82. Patience
    Prov. 27:1

Appendix II

How to Memorize Scripture

Often people come up to me after I preach and say, "My, you have a wonderful memory—I wish I could memorize like that! God has really gifted you with a great mind." I want to cry! Now do not misunderstand—I am what I am by the grace of God! (I Corinthians 15:10) Paul said, "For who maketh thee to differ from another? and what hast thou that thou didst not receive? now if thou didst receive it, why dost thou glory, as if thou hadst not received it?" (I Corinthians 4:7)

Usually, I respond to those comments with, "Well, I have a photo-graphic mind, but I ran out of film a couple of years ago." They laugh, and that's the end of the conversation. But before you read any further, let me share with you the real secret to memorizing Scripture—"time and work." Now don't stop reading, because I think in the next few minutes, I can make that "time" effective and the "work" enjoyable.

Let me tell you first how it all started with me. When I went to college I decided after an enjoyable freshman speech class to minor in it. I did it because I thought it would be fun, not because I thought I would ever use anything I was about to learn. Because of that minor in speech, I was required to be in the college dramas that were performed on campus twice each year as well as do poetry and monologues in various Vesper services and the like. I was also required to do a Recital at the end of my senior year. This required me to do a lot of memorizing. I was in the plays *As You Like It, Hamlet, The Robe, Julius Caesar*, and my favorite—*Cyrano*! My German nose helped me land that part! In *Cyrano* alone, I had over 1500 lines to memorize and as I always say, I had to know "when" to say them, so I had to memorize the lines just before mine too! For my recital, I did the comedy, *Teahouse of the August Moon*. I loved it all and would do it all again if I had the chance.

But by the time graduation rolled around, my brain was fried! It could not hold any more "memory," and so for the next four years, I did not conscientiously memorize anything! But, I was always convicted that I should be. I would listen to preachers quote portions of Scripture and think—I could do that. I was busy in revival work: writing sermons, preaching, winning souls, helping churches, being a husband and dad, etc., and so excused myself from any further discipline in the "study" area. But the Holy Spirit kept reminding me: "If you could memorize Shakespeare— you could memorize the Scripture."

In October of 1978, we were holding a Christian School revival in Coleman, Wisconsin. I preached several times during the school day to various age groups, but there were no services or activities in the evening. The town of Coleman at that time had a population of 300 and when five o'clock in the evening rolled around, the town shut down. Stores were not open, people disappeared from the streets, and everything became extremely quiet. I was bored to tears! My wife and I were traveling in a 25 foot trailer. Our oldest son, John, was just a little over a year old. The first night after supper, I went to the gym and shot some baskets for a couple of hours, but there's only so much fun you can have by yourself. Finally, after a couple of nights of this, I announced to Diane that I was going inside the school to memorize some Bible verses.

The only reason I did it was because I was bored and needed something to kill time. As I sat there that first night contemplating where to start, I realized that almost every week in revivals, I would preach a message on the subject of Hell. So, that's where I started. In the next couple of hours, I had memorized about ten verses on Hell and was pretty proud of myself. It was kind of fun to "preach" them as I would memorize them in the big gym that would make my voice sound more powerful than it was. I got so excited about it that the next night I went back inside and went at it again. By the end of that week, I had memorized about thirty verses on Hell, including the entire passage in Luke 16 about the rich man and Lazarus.

I really did not plan for it to go any further than that. I had killed some time with something profitable and knew that I would probably not have too many weeks where I would ever be that bored again. Our next revival was in Hadley, Michigan; and when we arrived, the pastor informed me that Monday evening would be Awana Parent's Night. He believed that several unsaved couples would be there to watch a short program and then hear me preach. I was excited about the opportunity to preach to a good number of lost people (there were eighteen visiting couples there that night), and I decided to preach on "Hell." But for the first time in my life, instead of reading the verses from the Bible in my message, I quoted them. I can't explain the power and life I felt in those words—which were not mine—but God's! For the first time in my ministry I felt like I was preaching "the Word."

I believe there were twelve adults who trusted Christ in that service! The next morning, I was up at four— memorizing verses—and I've been hooked on the power of God's Word ever since. But long before I ever discovered this potential—God wrote: "And these words, which I command thee this day, shall be in thine heart:" (Deuteronomy 6:6) "Therefore shall ye lay up these my words in your heart and in your soul … ." (Deuteronomy 11:18) "Thy word have I hid in my heart, that I might not sin against thee." (Psalm 119:11) "But what saith it? The word is nigh thee, even in thy mouth, and in thy heart: that is, the word of faith, which we preach." (Romans 10:8) "Let the word of Christ dwell in you richly… ." (Colossians 3:16)

Regardless of what this world teaches about success, God makes it clear that success only comes from one source: "This book of the law shall not depart out of thy mouth; but thou shalt meditate therein day and night, that thou mayest observe to do according to all that is written therein: for then thou shalt make thy way prosperous, and then thou shalt have good success." (Joshua 1:8) This is the only time you'll find the word "success" in the Bible and God states that it comes as a result of "meditating" on His Word. You can not meditate on something you haven't put in your heart!

There are many good "plans" out there to help you memorize, but let me share with you what has worked for me. It's a little bit unique, but remember—"time and work" are the key. The biblical principle is "what you sow is what you reap" so you'll get out of this in exact proportion to the time and energy you put in to it.

Choose A Specific Time And A Quiet Place

Very little gets accomplished in our lives that is not planned. If you are seriously going to memorize Scripture, you must be willing to block off a section of time when you are free from other distractions of life. I'm not talking about your commute drive here or time in the check-out line at Wal-Mart! I'm talking about time like Jesus spent alone in communion with His Father: "And in the morning, rising up a great while before day, he went out, and departed into a solitary place, and there prayed." (Mark 1:35) "And when he had sent the multitudes away, he went up into a mountain apart to pray: and when the evening was come, he was there alone." (Matthew 14:23)

Most of us today resist being "alone." We feel like we've always got to be in the middle of the action. May I say, that some of the loneliest people in the world are in the middle of a crowd. They are surrounded by people but are lonely. There is a huge difference between loneliness and solitude. Solitude is something you choose—and you better—if you plan to survive in this world. We need time with God and His Word "alone!"

You say, "You don't understand my world. I'm surrounded by people from the time I get up until I go to bed—my time is never my own." And I say, that's why you're frustrated and about to "burn out!" In Mark chapter one, Jesus was surrounded by people (read his schedule beginning in verse twenty one!) But the next morning, while everyone else was still asleep—He choose a solitary place—verse 35. Believe me, there is a time when no one else is up! You say, "But I'm not a morning person." You can become one. We're talking about success here rather than failure! Someone has said, "The difference between genius and average is what you do while every one else is sleeping!" Get up thirty minutes before everyone else does and see what a difference it will make in your spiritual life as you spend that time memorizing God's Word.

Organize By Topic

The purpose of memorization is to be able to recall Scripture when you need it, for the purpose you need it for. "For he mightily convinced the Jews, and that publickly, shewing by the scriptures that Jesus was Christ."(Acts 18: 28) The Bible covers hundreds of subjects and it is through these topics that it applies to our lives. (See Appendix I for a list of topics of sin and the Scriptures helping us to conquer those sins.) When Jesus was tempted by Satan in the wilderness (Matthew 4), He did not just throw out any old verse to overcome the temptation. He used specific Old Testament Scriptures that dealt with the temptation. When Satan tempted Him to turn the stones into bread to ease

His hunger, He quoted Deuteronomy 8:3: "…It is written, Man shall not live by bread alone, but by every word that proceedeth out of the mouth of God." (Matthew 4:4)

Choose a topic: It may be an area of sin that you are struggling with like pride, or selfishness, or maybe it's a subject you plan to preach on like Heaven or Hell. Get a concordance and look up that subject—you will find dozens of verses listed under the major topics of the Bible.

Get some cards and write the verses out on those "memory" cards. It doesn't matter what size you use—it depends on how good your eyes are. I used a small card about the size of a business card (a 4x6 index card cut into four equal parts). Writing the verses out on these cards is the first process of memorizing. I am aware that there are programs where you can buy the cards already printed. I had a pastor once ask me if he could "photocopy" my cards. I said, "Sure, but they'll never make it out of your desk drawer if you do." There is great value in writing the verses out in long hand. God commanded it to be done in the Old Testament. "And thou shalt write them upon the posts of thy house, and on thy gates." (Deuteronomy 6:9) "And it shall be, when he sitteth upon the throne of his kingdom, that he shall write him a copy of this law in a book out of that which is before the priests the Levites." (Deuteronomy 17:18) "And thou shalt write upon them all the words of this law, when thou art passed over, that thou mayest go in unto the land which the Lord thy God giveth thee, a land that floweth with milk and honey; as the LORD God of thy fathers hath promised thee… And thou shalt write upon the stones all the words of this law very plainly." (Deuteronomy 27:3,8)

In all of the sermon preparation, lecture notes, and writing that I have done over the years, I have never one time in my life, "cut and pasted" Scripture. Laugh if you want, but I just believe when God said to "Study to show thyself approved unto God…" He was not thinking about "point and click" "cut and paste!" There is a disciplined process in memorization and it starts with writing out the verses.

Now here is where my plan gets unique from others. When I decided to start memorizing seriously in 1978, I thought through how I was going to be using what I had memorized. I had two situations in my ministry where I most often needed to know the Bible—when I was preaching and when I was talking with people one-on-one in soulwinning or counseling. When I was preaching, I really didn't need to know the reference, because I could write that in my notes. I could write: Joshua 1:8 and if I had memorized the verse, seeing that reference would trigger it in my mind and I could quote it. But when I was talking with people personally, I really didn't need to know the verse, because I usually had my Bible with me and I could show them the verse (which is usually wise anyway in soulwinning), but I needed to know the reference so that I would know where to turn.

Most memory plans have cards with the reference on one side of the card and then you flip it over and the verse is written out on the reverse side. That's great, but it was not going to meet my need. So, I decided that I needed to memorize both the reference and the verse. I took my subject, such as "Hell" and found all of the verses in my concordance on that subject. I chose the ones I wanted to memorize and arranged them in chronological order (as they come in the Bible). This is already done in the concordance, but I chose to skip some and memorize others. I was now going to memorize that entire block of verses, in order as they come in the Bible, with both reference and the verse.

So, on the front of the card, I wrote "Hell #1" as illustrated below:

Front of the card:

> # Hell #1

When I flipped the card over, I wrote out the reference and the verse as illustrated:

Back of the card:

> **Psalm 9:17**
>
> **The wicked shall be turned into hell, and all the nations that forget God.**

As I memorized that subject, I memorized not only the verse but the reference with it. The first verse in that stack of cards then cued me to the second verse with its reference and text, and the second verse cued me to the third verse, etc. Thus, I memorized an entire block of verses together under one subject, all in order as they came in the Bible chronologically.

The second card in my series of verses on the subject of "Hell" looked like this:

Front of the card:

Hell #2

Back of the card:

Matthew 3:12
Whose fan is in his hand, and he will throughly purge his floor, and gather his wheat into the garner; but he will burn up the chaff with unquenchable fire.

This method creates a catalog of verses in your mind under various topics and you are able to use them to apply to needs at any time. For the soulwinner, if someone you meet says, "Well, I don't believe in a place called Hell!" Immediately, you know right where to take him in the Bible and show him the evidence of God's Word. For the preacher or teacher, as you are preparing a sermon or lesson, and the text you are preaching deals with a specific subject, immediately you have your own "mental concordance" on that subject to draw from. (Here is where all that time you thought you were wasting by "writing and memorizing verses" is going to come back and save you hours of searching for just the right verse.) Suppose you are memorizing more than one verse in a row. For example, let's say you are on the subject of "Hell" and you want to memorize Luke 16:19-31, which is the story of the rich man and Lazarus. On the front of the card, you put "Hell #8, or whatever number it is in your sequence. On the back you write: Luke 16:19-31. Get as many of the verses as you can on that first card and then start a second card. On the front of it you would put "Hell #8b" and continue the text on the back. If you need a third card, it would be "Hell #8c," and so on.

Now you have your stack of cards. You may have selected five or ten under a particular topic or hundreds—it all depends on how comprehensive you want to be. Just remember, you are doing this so you can use it—not just to see how many you can memorize. This is not VBS—there are no ribbons—this is ministry—but there are rewards!

Let us start memorizing. We have got our tool—now let us make it work!

Work Out Loud

This is why we have chosen a quiet place, alone. This is part of the process that works. You see, God emphasizes "hearing" His Word. "But he said, Yea rather, blessed are they that hear the word of God and keep it." (Luke 11:28) "Therefore whosoever heareth these sayings of mine, and doeth them, I will liken him unto a wise man, which built his house upon a rock:" (Matthew 7:24) "He that hath an ear, let him hear what the Spirit saith unto the churches." (Revelation 3:22)

You have read it, written it out, now you are "hearing it," as phrase by phrase you commit it to memory. Some verses are easier to memorize than others so do not get frustrated. Keep going over pieces of the verse at a time and then adding more to it—always repeating all of it out loud. No secrets here—this takes time—but look at it as an investment. God said: "For the merchandise of it is better than the merchandise of silver, and the gain thereof than fine gold. She is more precious than rubies: and all the things thou canst desire are not to be compared unto her." (Proverbs 3:14-15) He adds in verse 18: "… and happy is every one that retaineth her."

Walk while you Memorize

Your body has rhythm. I'm sure you can tell who is coming down the hall of your house by their walk. Little children are able to memorize the words to songs long before they can read because the words are written to the rhythm of music. I can guarantee that you will memorize Scripture faster walking than sitting in a chair (or behind the wheel of your car stuck in rush hour traffic).

I was preaching at a teen camp one summer. I came out of my room and there was a young girl about fifteen sitting on a rock with her Bible in her lap and she was crying. I went over to her to see what was the matter. She said: "I've been trying to memorize this verse for the last thirty minutes and I just can't get it!" (She was trying to earn points for her team.) I took her Bible from her asking which verse it was that she was struggling with? I said, "Let me hear what you've got so far." Quite honestly, she did not have much.

She stammered through the first couple of words and got stuck. I must admit it was a rather difficult verse. I said: "Stand up." I pointed to a trailer about 50 yards down the sidewalk from where we were standing. "Take the Bible and walk toward that trailer and come back. Do exactly what you have been trying to do to memorize the verse while you walk. I'll wait for you right here and when you get back, we'll see how much you know." She looked at me weird, but took off. She made it to the trailer and turned around (I could see her lips moving as she was mouthing the words), she got about ten feet from the trailer and began running toward me, yelling: "I've got it! I've got it!" Sure enough, she did too. Now granted, she had been working on it before my experiment, but the walking sealed it.

Try it—the exercise will not hurt you either. I have been in small guest quarters at times and had only enough space to take three or four steps and turn around and walk back, but it makes all the difference in the world.

The rhythm in your body will make the verse not only a part of your mind but also a part of your entire being. And later, when you use it in preaching or teaching, it will come alive—it will become as I like to say—"animated." One of my great concerns is that the average person in the world today thinks the Bible is some stuffy book written centuries ago with no relativity to man today. When you quote it, and your whole body language is a part of what you are saying, the Word becomes alive! People sense its power and authority—its "Thus saith the Lord."

I must warn you here though. When you go to use it, you will have a hard time standing still. It is very difficult for me to stand behind the pulpit when I quote Scripture. I memorized it on the move and so my body wants to go! But, oh, the freedom of being able to move away from the pulpit and your notes and look into the eyes of your audience and "preach the Word!"

Review, Review, Review

Repetition is the key to learning. Some memory plans will tell you that if you say the verse a certain number of times for a certain number of days, you'll never forget it. That does not seem to work for me. I have to keep reviewing every verse. I have often stated, "We've all had more than one telephone number in our life, but we probably only remember the one we are using now." Use it or lose it, as they say. Until you have learned your entire stack of verses under a subject, you will need to go through all of them every day. Once you have that whole topic memorized, you may be able to reduce your review of that subject to once a week. Perhaps later, less, but you will have to keep going over them.

I figured it out one day. For every verse I have memorized over these years, counting all of the time it took to write out the verse, the memorization time and the review time, I have spent 200 hours on every verse that I have memorized! Now do you still think I have a photographic memory? I mean, really—I could teach a bad parrot to quote a verse in 200 hours! Do not tell me you just can not memorize or you are too old or whatever. You can, but like I said, it is "time and work."

Set Goals of Time

Once you start memorizing and using God's Word, you will not be able to get the verses written on cards fast enough. Let me caution you. Do not set a goal of how many verses you want to memorize in a day, week, month or year. The truth is some passages are much easier to memorize than others. You are already familiar with them, or they are narrative or story-type in nature and thus the material flows very easily and logically. Others are not like that. The biblical wording is sometimes different than the way we might say it today, and the sentence might be compounded in nature. You might spend several days on one verse. You will get discouraged if you set your goals on the number of verses. Set a goal of the amount of "time" you are going to spend daily, weekly, monthly, on memorization. Commit yourself to that time no matter what; and as you do, the number of verses will add up over the months and years.

In conclusion, let me say that some of the most enjoyable times of my life have been spent alone memorizing God's Word. In the wee hours of the morning, just God and me with His Word, putting into my life, something that He went to a lot of trouble to give to me. I have found that He has blessed that effort.

Oh, how I have enjoyed seeing God use it. I have a message that I call the "Scripture Sermon" that is forty-five minutes of solid Scripture—no references, no comments—just the pure Word of God. How I have enjoyed seeing God bless that. My friend, "Preach the Word!" You can not beat it!

Notes

Introduction:
[1] Haddon W. Robinson, *Biblical Preaching*, Grand Rapids, Michigan, Baker Book House, 1980, p. 18.
[2] Harold T. Bryson, *Expository Preaching*, Nashville, Tennessee, Broadman and Holman Publishers, 1995, p. 2.
[3] Ibid, p. 2.
[4] Ibid, p. 3.
[5] Lloyd M. Perry, *Biblical Sermon Guide*, Grand Rapids, Michigan, Baker Book House, 1970, preface.
[6] C. H. Spurgeon, *Lectures to my Students*, Grand Rapids, Michigan, Zondervan Publishing House, 1954, p. 7.

Chapter One:
[7] Phillips Brooks, *Homiletics*, New York, New York, E.P. Dutton and Company, 1877, p. 10.

[8] James Stalker, *The Preacher and his Models*, New York, New York, George H. Doran Company, 1891, p. 50.
[9] Henry Ward Beecher, *Yale Lectures on Preaching*, Boston, Massachusetts, The Pilgrim Press, 1872, pp. 38-39.
[10] Spurgeon, p. 8.
[11] Spurgeon, p. 11.
[12] Spurgeon, pp. 9-10.
[13] Stalker, pp. 267-272

Chapter Two:
[14] Robinson, pp. 53-54.
[15] Spurgeon, pp. 93-94.
[16] H.C. Brown Jr., H. Gordon Clinard, Jesse J. Northcutt, Al Fasol, *Steps to the Sermon*, Nashville, Tennessee, Broadman & Holman Publishers, 1996, p. 28.
[17] Perry, pp. 17-18.
[18] Spurgeon, p. 85.
[19] Robinson, p. 24.
[20] Ibid, p. 29.
[21] Beecher, Volume III, pp 27-28.

Chapter Four:
[22] Robinson, p. 160.
[23] Jay E. Adams, *Preaching with Purpose*, Grand Rapids, Michigan, Zondervan Publishing House, 1982, pp. 59-60.
[24] Robinson, p. 167.

Chapter Five:
[25] Clovis G. Chappell, *Questions Jesus Asked*, New York, New York, Abingdon-Cokesbury, 1948, reprint edition, Grand Rapids, Michigan, Baker Book Publishers, 1974, p. 154.

[26] Robinson, p. 139.
[27] Ibid, p. 140.
[28] Alan H. Monroe, *Principles and Types of Speech*, p. 231.
[29] Robinson, p. 143.
[30] John Hercus, *David*, Chicago, Illinois, Inter-Varisty Press, 1968, pp. 55-56.

Chapter Six:
[31] Spurgeon, pp. 349-353.
[32] Beecher, Volume I, p. 154.
[33] Perry G. Downs, *Teaching for Spiritual Growth*, Grand Rapids, Michigan, Zondervan Publishing House, 1994, pp. 64-65.
[34] Beecher, Volume I, p. 163.
[35] Beecher, Volume I, p. 173.
[36] Martyn Lloyd Jones, *Preachers and Preaching*, Grand Rapids, Michigan, Zondervan Publishing, 1971, pp. 224-243.

Chapter Seven:
[37] Robinson, p. 167.
[38] Adams, pp. 67, 69.
[39] Ibid, p.65
[40] Brown, Clinard, Northcutt, Fasol, p. 189.
[41] Robinson, p. 191.
[42] Spurgeon, pp. 111-112.

Chapter Eight:
[43] Charles R. Brown, *The Art of Preaching*, New York, New York, Macmillan Publishing Company, 1922, p.170.
[44] Spurgeon, p. 305.
[45] Ibid, p. 307.

[46] Richard Paget, *Human Speech: Some Observations, Experiments, and Conclusions as to the Nature, Origin, Purpose, and Possible Improvement of Human Speech*, New York, New York, Harcourt, Brace Publishing, 1930.
[47] Loren D. Reid, *Speaking Well*, Columbia, Missouri, Artcraft Publishing, 1962, p. 141.
[48] Spurgeon, pp. 284-285.
[49] Robinson, p. 198.
[50] John T. Molloy, *Dress for Success*, New York, New York, Wyden Publishers, 1975.
[51] Spurgeon, p. 286.

Chapter Nine:
[52] Spurgeon, p. 320

Chapter Ten:
[53] David H. Greer, *The Preacher and His Place*, New York, New York, University Press, 1895, pp. 243, 262-263.
[54] Stalker, pp. 199-202.
[55] Spurgeon, pp. 212-216.
[56] Beecher, pp. 300-301.

Chapter Eleven:
[57] Spurgeon, p. 188.
[58] Ibid, p. 193.
[59] Ibid, pp. 199-202.
[60] Downs, pp. 34, 54, 55, 200.
[61] Spurgeon, p. 204.

Bibliography

Adams, Jay. *Preaching With Purpose*. Grand Rapids, Michigan. Zondervan Publishing House. 1982.

Baird, James E. *Preparing for Platform and Pulpit*. Grand Rapids, Michigan. Baker Book House. 1976.

Barnhouse, Donald Grey. *Teaching the Word of Truth*. Philadelphia, Pennsylvania. Revelation Book Service. 1940.

Baxter, Batsell Barrett. *The Heart of the Yale Lectures*. Grand Rapids, Michigan. Baker Book House. 1971.

Beecher, Henry Ward. *Lectures on Preaching*. Boston, Massachusetts. Pilgrim Press. 1872.

Blackwood, Andrew Watterson. *Expository Preaching for Today*. Nashville, Tennessee. Abingdon-Cokesbury Press. 1946.

Blackwood, Andrew Watterson. *The Fine Art of Preaching*. New York, New York. McMillan Company. 1945.

Braga, James. *How To Prepare Bible Messages*. Portland, Oregon. Multnomah Press. 1969.

Breed, David R. *Preparing To Preach*. New York, New York. Hodder and Stoughton. 1911.

Broadus, John A. *On the Preparation and Delivery of Sermons*. New York, New York. Harper & Brothers. 1870.

Broadus, John A. *History of Preaching*. New York, New York. A.C. Armstrong and Sons. 1902.

Brooks, Phillips. *The Joy of Preaching*. Grand Rapids, Michigan. Kregel Publishers. 1989.

Brown, Charles Reynolds. *The Art of Preaching*. New York, New York. McMillan. 1924.

Brown, H.C. Jr. H. Gordon Clinard, Jesse J. Northcutt, Al Fasol. *Steps to the Sermon*. Nashville, Tennessee. Broadman & Holman Publishers. 1996.

Brown, H.C. *A Quest for Reformation in Preaching.* Waco, Texas. Word Books. 1968.

Bryson, Harold T. *Expository Preaching.* Nashville, Tennessee. Broadman & Holman Publishers. 1995.

Bryson, Harold T. and James C. Taylor. *Building Sermons to Meet People's Needs.* Nashville, Tennessee. Broadman Press. 1980.

Chappell, Bryan. *Christ-Centered Preaching.* Grand Rapids, Michigan. Baker Book House. 1994.

Cleland, James T. *Preaching to be Understood.* Nashville, Tennessee. Abingdon Press. 1965.

Daane, James. *Preaching with Confidence.* Grand Rapids, Michigan. Eerdmans Publishing Company. 1980.

Dale, R. W. *Nine Lectures on Preaching.* New York, New York. A. S. Banner & Company. 1877.

Downs, Perry G. *Teaching for Spiritual Growth.* Grand Rapids, Michigan. Zondervan Publishing House. 1994.

Evans, William. *How to Prepare Sermons.* Chicago, Illinois. Moody Press. 1964.

Fry, Jacob. *Elementary Homiletics.* Philadelphia, Pennsylvania. Board of Publishing of the General Council. 1904.

Garrison, Webb. B. *Creative Imagination in Preaching.* Nashville, Tennessee. Abingdon Press. 1960.

Garrison, Webb B. *The Preacher and his Audience.* New York, New York. Fleming H. Revell Company. 1954.

Gibbs, Alfred P. *The Preacher and his Preaching.* Fort Dodge, Iowa. Walterick Printing Company. 1939.

Graves, Mike. *The Sermon as a Symphony.* Valley Forge, Pennsylvania. Judson Press. 1977.

Greer, David H. *The Preacher and his Place.* New York, New York. University Press. 1895.

Hamilton, Donald L. *Homiletical Handbook.* Nashville, Tennessee. Broadman & Holman Press. 1992.

Henderson, George. *Lectures to Young Preachers.* Goodmayes, Essex. G. F. Vallance.

Hoyt, Arthur S. *Vital Elements of Preaching.* New York, New York. McMillan. 1923.

Hoyt, Arthur S. *The Work of Preaching.* New York, New York. McMillan. 1921.

Johnston, Graham. *Preaching to a Postmodern World.* Grand Rapids, Michigan. Baker Book House. 2001.

Jones, Martyn Lloyd. *Preachers and Preaching.* Grand Rapids, Michigan. Zondervan Publishing. 1971.

Jordan, G. Ray. *You Can Preach.* New York, New York. Fleming H. Revell Company. 1951.

Koller, Charles W. *How To Preach Without Notes.* Grand Rapids, Michigan. Baker Book House. 1962.

Kroll, Woodrow Michael. *Prescription For Preaching.* Grand Rapids, Michigan. Baker Book House. 1980.

Larsen, David L. *The Anatomy of Preaching.* Grand Rapids, Michigan. Kregel Publishing. 1989.

Logan, Samuel T. *The Preacher and Preaching.* Phillipsburg, New Jersey. Presbyterian and Reformed Publishing Company. 1986.

McCracken, Robert J. *The Making of a Sermon.* New York, New York. Harper and Brothers. 1956.

McDill, Wayne. *The 12 Essential Skills for Great Preaching.* Nashville, Tennessee. Broadman & Holman. 1994.

Miller, Calvin. *Spirit, Word, and Story.* Grand Rapids, Michigan. Baker Book House. 1996.

Miller, Calvin. *The Empowered Communicator.* Nashville, Tennessee. Broadman & Holman. 1994.

Moorehead, Lee C. *Freedom of the Pulpit.* Nashville, Tennessee. Abingdon Press. 1961.

Morgan, G. Campbell. *Preaching.* London, England. Marshall, Morgan, and Scott. 1937.

Olford, David L. *A Passion for Preaching.* Nashville, Tennessee. Thomas Nelson Publishing. 1989.

Pattison, T. Harwood. *The Making of a Sermon.* Philadelphia, Pennsylvania. American Baptist Publication Society. 1898.

Patton, Carl S. *The Preparation and Delivery of Sermons.* Chicago, Illinois. Willet, Clark and Company. 1938.

Patton, Carl S. *The Use of the Bible in Preaching.* Chicago, Illinois. Willet, Clark, and Company. 1936.

Perry, Lloyd M. *A Manual for Preaching.* Grand Rapids, Michigan. Baker Book House. 1965.

Perry, Lloyd M. *Biblical Sermon Guide.* Grand Rapids, Michigan. Baker Book House. 1970.

Pierson, Arthur T. *The Divine Art of Preaching.* New York, New York. Baker and Taylor Company. 1892.

Pitt-Watson, Ian. *A Primer for Preachers.* Grand Rapids, Michigan. Baker Book House. 1986.

Ramesh, Richard. *Scripture Sculpture.* Grand Rapids, Michigan. Baker Book House. 1995.

Riley, W.B. *The Preacher and his Preaching.* Murfreesboro, Tennessee. Sword of the Lord Publishing. 1948. Reprint 1996. St. John, Indiana. Christian Book Gallery.

Ripley, Henry T. *Sacred Rhetoric.* Boston, Massachusetts. Gould and Lincoln. 1862.

Robinson, Haddon W. *Biblical Preaching.* Grand Rapids, Michigan. Baker Book House. 1980.

Robinson, Haddon W. *Making a Difference in Preaching.* Grand Rapids, Michigan. Baker Book House. 1999.

Roddy, Clarence Stonelynn. *We Prepare and Preach.* Chicago, Illinois. Moody Press. 1959.

Sangster, W. E. *The Craft of Sermon Construction.* Grand Rapids, Michigan. Baker Book House. 1951.

Simpson, Matthew. *Lectures on Preaching.* New York, New York. Phillips and Hunt. 1879.

Smith, Arthur H. *Preachers and Preaching.* Philadelphia, Pennsylvania. United Lutheran Publishing House. 1925.

Spurgeon, C.H. *Lectures to my Students*. Grand Rapids, Michigan. Zondervan Publishing House. 1954.

Stalker, James. *The Preacher and his Models*. New York, New York. Hodder and Stoughton Publishing. 1891.

Tatford, Fredrick A. *The Art of Preaching*. Kilmarnock, Scotland. John Ritchie Publishers. 1932.

Tizard, Leslie J. *Preaching: The Art of Communication*. New York, New York. Oxford University Press. 1959.

Unger, Merrill F. *Principles of Expository Preaching*. Grand Rapids, Michigan. Zondervan. 1955.

Welt, Don De. *If You Want To Preach*. Grand Rapids, Michigan. Baker Book House. 1957.

Willhite, Keith and Scott Gibson. *The Big Idea of Preaching*. Grand Rapids, Michigan. Baker Book House. 1998.

White, Douglas M. *The Excellence of Exposition*. Neptune, New Jersey. Lizeaux Brothers. 1977.

Whitesell, Faris D. *Power in Expository Preaching*. New York, New York. Fleming H. Revell Company. 1943.

Wiersbe, Warren W. *The Dynamics of Preaching*. Grand Rapids, Michigan. Baker Book House. 1999.

Zinchke, F. Barnham. *The Duty and Discipline of Expository Preaching*. London, England. Rivingtons Publishers. 1866.